Praise for *Running Towa*

"Our effort, hours of work, dedication, and love for what [we] (Livermore) and I were doing jumped off the pages and smacked me right in my heart. I sure wasn't expecting that."

—Shannon Yewell Weil, one of the founders of the Western States Endurance Run

"Thank you for including my Dad (Northern Nevada ultra-running legend Roland Martin) in your project. You brought his essence to light. Your writing is something special."

—Jenny Capel, champion ultramarathon runner and longtime northern Nevada running organizer and volunteer

"The author's concise history of the sport is both rigorously researched and affectingly personal—the peek he provides is from an enthusiastic participant in a little-known cosmos. In addition, he poses a convincing argument that athletic achievement can be 'uplifting and soul-affirming' rather than merely an exercise in Type A vanity. Trent's remembrance is an intelligently meditative one as well as historically edifying. An insightful tour of an intense athletic world unknown to most."

—from *Kirkus Reviews*

"Dedicated to endurance runs, [Trent] recounts a lifetime dream of completing a 100-mile distance run, sharing the ups and downs that led to his accomplishment of that dream as well as his injuries and setbacks along the way. Trent's appraisal of the immense physical challenges of ultrarunning is just the start: he also shares the spotlight with his mentors and running companions who motivated him to go the distance during the journey."

—from *BookLife Reviews*

"But beyond its personal and sports-historical elements, the book also includes self-help elements for other athletes, with advice on finding mentors and overcoming challenges. Its chapters are topical, musing on subjects like 'the magic of the golden hour' in an inspirational manner and sharing details about how ultra runners stay motivated to keep going through pain. Trent lays bare the mindsets of those who push themselves to physical extremes, musing on what motivates distance runners and about what affirmations ultra running provides."

—from *Foreword Reviews*

RUNNING
TOWARD LIFE

Broad Book Press, Publisher

Paperback ISBN: 978-1-7375178-2-5

eBook ISBN: 978-1-7375178-3-2

Published in the United States by Broad Book Press, an imprint of Broad Book Group, Edwardsville, IL.

Book Design & Production: Vicky Vaughn Shea, Ponderosa Pine Design

Icon art: iStock.com/etraveler

Library of Congress Control Number: 2022920739

RUNNING
TOWARD LIFE

FINDING COMMUNITY AND WISDOM
IN THE DISTANCES WE RUN

JOHN **TRENT**

broad
book
press

Table of **Contents**

Introduction

I WILL NEVER FORGET the events of June 24-25, 1995.

It was on that weekend that I ran 38 miles and became an ultra mara-thoner. I find it personally comforting and altogether appropriate given how the intervening decades have played out, that if you went search-ing for my result, you would never find it. I ran that day as a "pacer" for my friend Joe Braninburg, who was 51 at the time and gunning for a top-10 finish at the Western States Endurance Run. For years, Western States, one of the world's first and arguably most well-known mountain hundred-milers (first held officially in 1977), defined a "pace runner" as "a trail companion who may accompany a runner along designated sections of the trail. Pacers are allowed solely as a safety consideration for fatigued runners in the remote and rugged territory of the Western States Trail." When I joined Joe on a sweltering afternoon at the 62-mile mark at Foresthill School, the day would see temperatures soar to 104 degrees, still the hottest day ever recorded at Western States. The plan was to run the final 38 miles for a newspaper story I was writing for my employer at the time, the *Reno Gazette-Journal*.

Before he even got to the tiny town of Foresthill, California at about 5:30 p.m., or about 12½ hours after starting the race, Joe and the rest of the 360-plus runners had skimmed, slipped, slid, and fallen over the first 24 miles of the course, which was treacherously covered in snow and ice courtesy of an endless, record-setting Sierra winter. Now it was my job to serve as Joe's shadow for the final 38 miles. The navy blue Ultimate Direction fanny pack I wore overflowed like a picnic basket from the overthinking that comes when you have no idea what you are doing and what might lie ahead. My pack holstered two constantly sloshing 12-ounce water bottles. There were four Power Bars tucked tightly inside one of the pack's pockets. Like everything else that oppressive day, the contents quickly melted from the heat and were reduced to a gooey mess, streaking my hands yellow whenever I took a bite from them. I packed two six-inch, AA-battery-powered flashlights I'd purchased from Wal-Mart a few days before. My lights were about as sturdy as a couple of glass test tubes. I'd never run at night with flashlights. I had no idea if they would be strong enough. As the sun dropped and the night running began, the lights were tossed around inside my fanny pack, quickly sounding like loose marbles inside a tin can, shattered to pieces from the hard and aggressive running Joe would do on a surprisingly rocky and technical trail.

And, even more important than the water and the sticky Power Bars and the lights that were crushed to pieces, I made sure to carry with me the tools of my sportswriter trade—a classic, Pitman-ruled, 4-by-8-inch, 70-sheet, spiraled, and essentially palm-sized reporter's notebook, along with two black ballpoint pens. Every few miles, whenever Joe would cruise into an aid station, or maybe the few times when he would stop running and methodically hike like a man on a mission, his powerful, tanned, and sun-freckled contractor's arms pumping with purpose up a hill, I would pull out my notebook and one of my pens and madly jot down the details of what I was experiencing. The famed sportswriter W.C. "Bill" Heinz once remarked that quoting someone is like walking on thin ice: "You go gently so you don't break through." There was nothing gentle to my note taking that day. My arms and hands flowed with sweat that wouldn't stop. More than a few times, my pen slipped right out of my fingers and fell to the ground, disappearing into a tiny mushroom cloud of trail dust. The sweat on my hands soaked the pages of my notebook into near-incomprehensibility. With each note I'd attempt to record, the page became stubborn, surfeited with my sweat, almost as if it were refusing the ink. The dialogue and details of a run that felt increasingly epic to me were being translated onto the pages of my notebook in black smudges and streaks. The frantic fragments of memory that I'd managed to scrawl out came in between fitful bouts of muttering under my breath and trying not to trip and fall on a trail that seemed to have cruel intentions for my well-being.

Looking back on it now, beyond the fact that it was a minor miracle that I could even read my notes afterward, I wasn't just noting the critical moments of an amazing race that would see Joe become one of the few over-50 runners to ever finish in the top 10 at Western States. He would do so heroically, summoning a strong surge just past the 90-mile mark, passing two of the famed Tarahumara runners from the Sierra Madre Occidental of northwestern Mexico. He splashed determinedly by them through a slippery creek bed, sending the cold California Gold Country water fishtailing crazily behind him, to move from 12th place to 10th place. The presence of the Tarahumara runners gave meaning and haunting sound to the experience. The Tarahumara were an Indigenous people who could trace their relationship with running back centuries. They were legendary for having worn rawhide sandals and having the ability to run for miles from their enclave of hillside caves. The Tarahumara that Joe chased that sweltering June were lithe and moved with the effortlessness of clouds moving across the sky. I will never forget their sound, the only thing that betrayed their presence on the trail. There was the almost imperceptible slapping of their sandals ("huaraches," no longer made from plants or animals but from the rubber of tires) against the trail, which was so light it was like a pleasing murmur or a soft breeze. The white tunics they wore were cinched tightly around their stout waists with metal bells, which, when worn during their persistence hunts of long ago, were said to fill the Tarahumara with the speed of the deer they were hunting. As we had given them chase, we could hear the bells of the Tarahumara on the switchbacks down below us, rising mystically up through the muggy night air as if from a different place and a different time, their sound beckoning us to run as they did. Once Joe sped past the two Tarahumara through that creek bed, for nearly a half mile after, we could hear the bells behind us, the beat quickening as the Tarahumara gave chase. It was a soundtrack of pure competitive effort that made me want to linger and listen in the way that beautiful music always makes us yearn for a great song to keep going and never to end. Joe, of course, wasn't feeling nearly as reflective as I was. He determinedly kept pushing the pace. His sole motivation was to out-run the sound of the Tarahumara. Gradually, the haunting bells that I can still close my eyes and hear nearly 30 years later faded into the night behind us.

Joe would eventually get his 10th-place finish. He would finish in 20 hours, 55 minutes, and 26 seconds. It was a day that saw one of the highest drop-out rates in Western States history. Only 53.4 percent of the race's more than 360 starters would complete the 100.2-mile trek from Olympic Valley, California to the Placer High School track in Auburn, California. And if there was any question if the experience, on a day that would become known in Western States lore as the "The Year of Ice and Fire," was worthwhile for Joe, that was quickly answered only a few seconds after he had crossed the finish line. Joe's girlfriend at the time handed him a sealed manila envelope, which Joe promptly passed on to a surprised but smiling race director Norman Klein. Puzzled, Norm opened the envelope. Inside was a $165 check and completed entry form for the next year's Western States. This was a race, as I was to find out in my own experience, that was impossible to simply be one-and-done with.

I recorded all of those sounds and scenes in a sweaty, messy, excited, and entirely insufficient scrawl. I remember thinking, as I sat at my computer terminal in the RGJ's newsroom the next day trying to decipher the trail cacophony of my handwritten notes running up and sliding down the pages, that what I had experienced was something I would always remember. But it was more than that. To that point in my life, I had run 10K's, half-marathons, and marathons. The standard 26.2-mile distance had always seemed as far as I would've ever wished to run. Then, pacing Joe, I had run as far as I had ever run in my life— 38 miles. As I pored over my notes and attempted to compose my story in the air-conditioned comfort of a quiet newsroom a little less than 12 hours after having paced Joe, shifting my weight about every five minutes or so to minimize the stiffness that was raging through my battered quads and burning hips, I felt as if my horizons as a runner had suddenly, substantially, and inescapably broadened. I was no longer a runner. I was now an ultra runner, even if it hadn't been my race that I had finished. In fact, it was an almost instantaneous innermost desire I felt as I sat there that Sunday afternoon, writing about how someone else had gone the great 100-mile distance. As I was composing Joe's story, I was gripped with a surprising sense of wanting to embark, someday soon, on a 100-mile journey of my own. From that day forward, I wanted to be an ultra runner. Continuing to this day, I have been an ultra runner. My experience in the sport started by bearing testimony to an amazing run by a 51-year-old man. Today, this is my testimony. I am the possessor of tens of thousands of trail miles, finishes in nearly 100 ultra-marathon races (including 17 hundred-milers), and, perhaps most importantly of all, a better and abiding sense of who I am.

Ultra running has taught me lessons that I don't know I could've understood in any other context. I've come to understand, through a lot of trial, error, and unending belief in the good that is inherent in the sport, that going the distance only tells part of the story. Who we are and what we determine to be important is always magnified by the great distances we run. I am convinced that we acquire experiences—either our own or those that we share with our friends whom we crew and pace—that make us better people, or at least remind us that the best lives lived make us strive and aspire to be better people. They make us do our best to contribute in some small way—as participants, as volunteers, as supporters of the dreams of our friends, as members of trail crews—to the wonderfully eclectic community of ultra runners who are spread out throughout the country and the world. Ultra running has made me feel more connected with who I hope to be. It has filled me with more of a common purpose, more of a willingness to take a chance. It has allowed me to expose my deepest feelings for people to view in plain sight and to nurture the shared humanity that resides in us all.

In 1997, two years after my experience running with and being inspired by Joe, I ran my first Western States. Although the race has a 30-hour time limit, many entrants shoot for the "stretch" goal of finishing the race in a little less than a day, in under 24 hours. If you finish in under 24 hours, you receive what is considered one of the most coveted finisher's awards in all of running, an exquisite hand-crafted silver belt buckle produced by a family-owned business, Comstock Heritage. I wrote another newspaper story about that 1997 experience, one that if it had followed the perfect script that day would've seen me triumphantly finish in under 24 hours. The crescendo would have been a few hours later during the awards ceremony, when I would've been presented with one of those beautiful silver belt buckles.

It didn't happen that way. Just as I had two years earlier with Joe, I had run further that day in 1997 than I had ever run in my life:

100.2 miles. But I had somehow come up short. I finished in 24 hours, 1 minute, and 36 seconds. I missed a silver belt buckle, with the words "100 MILES ONE DAY" emblazoned across it by a mere 96 seconds. The solemn finality of those words that had tantalized me throughout months of hard training and seemed to immortalize those who were lucky enough to achieve it had evaded me. I received instead a bronze buckle, with the simple words "100 MILES." To my way of thinking then, "100 MILES ONE DAY" sounded much more substantial and fuller of triumph than the more restrained, "100 MILES."

This may sound strange, but not reaching the sub-24-hour milestone that day was probably the best thing that could have ever happened to me. In the wake of the 1997 Western States, I was determined to dust myself off, swallow my injured pride, and try the 100-mile distance again. I felt this way because the experience, though it didn't achieve a goal, taught me something much more important. I met people that day whom I have never forgotten. Among the most memorable was 57-year-old Gary Ritchie from Sacramento. Gary was a cancer survivor. He ran that day, proudly, in a pair of red, white, and blue USA shorts, as a man who was incredibly grateful to be alive. Gary was a well-known and respected person in the ultra community. As Gary ran into each of Western States' more than 20 aid stations, he seemed to know everybody. He was greeted with raucous cheers, as a hometown hero whose grit and tenacity in overcoming cancer was not only well-known but revered. There were moments where it seemed that Gary was the most popular runner in the world. At one point, I trailed behind Gary as he swept into the Dusty Corners aid station near mile 38. Volunteers and friends swarmed him like he was a wildly popular presidential candidate during primary season. It was miraculous that Gary actually extricated himself from the Dusty Corners people, all of whom offered hugs and handshakes and wanted to wish Gary well. By contrast, I remember being pretty much forgotten as I chugged into the aid station behind Gary. Such was the wattage of a man who was clearly loved by everyone. I stood by myself, left alone to pour my own cup of Coke, and watched with a mix of awe and envy as Gary was given the royal Dusty Corners treatment.

Gary, like me, just missed finishing in under 24 hours. He finished about five minutes behind me. I remember how crushed I felt as I stood at the finish line on the Placer High School track. I fought the urge to cry. But eventually I couldn't help myself and was bawling in front of my wife, Jill, our two young daughters Annie and Katie and several of my friends who had helped that day. Gary and I had run parts of about 50 miles that day together. After he finished, Gary made it a point to put his disappointment of breaking 24 hours behind him and to put the moment into its proper place. In his life, Gary had faced challenges far greater than missing a time goal by a few insignificant minutes. I was 34 years old at the time. Gary was about the same age as I am now. He did what all people who have experienced the difficulties and triumphs and tragedies of life should always do with people who haven't lived as long and who haven't had the life experience they have had. Gary slipped through my family and friends, stood next to me, and smiled like a proud father. He gave me a hug. He said, "You gave it all you had, John. That's all we can ever ask of ourselves."

Gary's story, like so many other stories since then, has clung to me, reminding me that there are important lessons we can take from our time on the trail. For a long time after my Western States experience in 1997, I kept the cotton socks that I wore that day pinned like a prized fresco to one of the walls of our garage. The socks were stained by the peach-colored dust of 24 hours, 1 minute, and 36 seconds of what felt like deeply disappointing running on the Western States Trail. But as the days passed after that initial disappointment, I came to look at the socks as less tinged with 96 seconds of competitive failure and more colored by the grace and goodness of 100.2 miles of human experience. The dust of the trail that my socks had collected was just like the stories and the special people that I'd experienced and collected along the way that day. Looking back on it now, it was a day that felt like it had been filled with a thrilling electrical shock . . . before everything went completely to black just 96 seconds short of my goal. Eventually, even the 96 seconds where I fell short came to represent a certain determination and defiance. I was far from being done. I would try to run 100 miles again. And eventually I would finish. Again. And again. And again. There were many more days still to come that would be much more uplifting and soul-affirming. But the point was becoming clear. Every time I'd pull something out of my garage, I couldn't help but stare at my Western States socks with wonder and a small bit of pride. This was a sport that was sticking to me. It was becoming a part of who I was.

My hope in writing this book, which is loosely divided into three parts all speaking to various points of development in one's running life, "Finding Your Mentors," "Choosing Your Companions," and "Overcoming Your Challenges," is that those who read it will come away with a similar sense of understanding of who they are and what is important to them. Although these stories are highly personal, they contain some of the larger truths that we all experience in our lives. That we are constantly learning and evolving. That as time passes and as we accrue thousands of hard-earned miles on the trails, there are important lessons that are equally hard-earned and can stick with us if we allow them to live on. And that as we gain these experiences, we come to view them more like a way station and not a final destination, where we have the opportunity to continually ask ourselves important questions that help us grow and learn. No matter what distance of ultra we run, we come to understand that whenever we go the distance, it isn't just the number of miles that we have run that matter. As I found out in 1995, you can run an ultra distance that comes on the periphery of something larger and it may not ever be remembered—except by you. Running ultras is a way of running toward what matters most: understanding and finding a greater meaning in the life that we live. It helps us run toward our lives.

PART **ONE**:

Finding Your
Mentors

CHAPTER 1

The Making of a
Writer and a Runner

Mrs. Shineesta Williams was the type of person that you quickly made note of and never forgot. I had the good fortune of being in Mrs. Williams' sixth grade class at Stead Elementary School during the 1974-75 academic year. Students at Stead Elementary knew ahead of time who the good teachers were. There were those who were so mean and strict the entire experience was miserable. There were those who were too soft who didn't push their students enough. And there were those who were masters, who taught in such a way that there was always a delicate balance between discipline and direction, just enough of both to make the school year productive and worthwhile. Mrs. Williams was at the top of everyone's list. I remember the excitement I felt that September as I sat in Mrs. Williams' classroom, wondering just what it was about this woman that made her such a great teacher.

Mrs. Williams was probably in her early 50s then, with short gray hair that was on its way to becoming white, with a few remnants of the black hair she had as a young woman still visible, giving her a wise but also energetic quality. Her face was a map of her journeys and travels, with deep lines etched across her forehead and equally deep lines running down from her cheeks, like paths that had crossed and would one day cross again.

Stead, the former Air Force base lined with hunching sagebrush and dry lake beds located about 12 miles north of Reno, where I had grown up, wasn't a place where people dressed extravagantly. It was a middle- to lower-middle-class community where poorly paid college professors like my father lived next door to families whose head of the household had gone directly from their service in World War II as Navy Seabees (and still had the Seabee tattoos on their forearms to prove it) into carpentry or construction. The mothers of our neighborhood rarely wore dresses, opting instead for shorts in the summer and bell legged jeans or polyester slacks in the winter. Mrs. Williams almost always wore dresses and skirts that were colorful and that felt full of life and seemed to reflect a teaching career of great variety that reached from her home state of Oklahoma to the desert southwest of Arizona and now Nevada. Her long, thin, and expressive hands and wrists were always adorned with all types of turquoise and silver jewelry. Fashions always change, of course, and I'm sure that some of what Mrs. Williams wore would probably feel dated today. But sitting in her classroom on that first day and continuing on through the school year, I remember always feeling so impressed by the timelessness of her manner. With everything that she wore, and with all of her interactions with her students, which never felt wasted and always had an extremely focused sense of purpose, there was a proud and confident quality to everything that Mrs. Williams did.

Mrs. Williams was Native American, a member of the Chickasaw Nation of Oklahoma. The students of Stead Elementary all knew about Mrs. Williams' heritage. I had never met any Native Americans to this point in my life. I wondered how or if Mrs. Williams would incorporate her experiences into what she taught us. As it turned out, Mrs. Williams, like so many teachers of that era, was more concerned, on the first day and in the first hours of our school year together, with simply teaching us. It wasn't about her; it was about all of us. Mrs. Williams never lost sight of this ultimate goal. She very deliberately, patiently, and masterfully taught us more in that year than any of us could have ever imagined. Because of this, my classmates and I never lost sight of how lucky we were to be in her presence. I would only get small hints, occasional mentions, an off-handed comment or two, followed by one of Mrs. Williams' warm and welcoming smiles, of what her life had been like.

My sense was that hers was a good life. Mrs. Williams' husband, Mr. Barry "Buck" Williams, who wasn't Native American, was also a teacher at Stead Elementary. Mrs. Williams' voice was always soft and comforting, delivered through carefully chosen words that were liberating in how well they were spoken, each word always unlocking a door of learning you hadn't known existed. Mr. Williams' voice was something completely different. He spoke in an Oklahoma drawl that felt like it was an entertaining mashup of words that were all cousins to one another, close enough in meaning and in sound to rapidly get his point across to you. Although he sounded folksy, Mr. Williams, who wore black horn-rimmed glasses, had a shaved head, and usually wore white short-sleeved shirts with ties, was an extremely well-read and engaging person. There was a lunch hour where Mr. Williams had lunch duty in the cafeteria, and he recited lines from the 1913 limerick written by the reporter and poet Dixon Lanier Merritt about pelicans: "A wonderful bird is the pelican/His bill will hold more than his belican." There were the other lunch hours when Mrs. Williams would sometimes let me stay in the classroom to work on my writing while she would eat lunch at her desk with her husband. Those were the moments, as I would write for a few minutes, then eavesdrop a bit, where I heard more about Mrs. Williams' life—the latest activities of Mr. and Mrs. Williams' college-aged son and high school-aged daughter, an occasional mention of "Chilocco" (the Chilocco Indian School, where Mrs. Williams had graduated high school in 1942 and later taught at) or "Chickasha" (the small Oklahoma town where Mr. and Mrs. Williams had grown up, became sweethearts, and married in 1947).

Those lunch hours. They became incredibly important to me. Not just to see a happily married teaching couple sweetly enjoying sandwiches and potato chips together during the noon hour at the school where they taught, but for what that 55-minute period of time came to mean to me. I was discovering that I was a writer. Very early on in the school year, Mrs. Williams began encouraging me about my writing. I enjoyed all aspects of our afternoons, when the class would shift to English and Mrs. Williams would spend equal amounts of time teaching us the rudiments of grammar and then either reading to us or having us read quietly to ourselves. Watching Mrs. Williams diagram a sentence was a thing of beauty. She likened the exercise to cooking: "A recipe is not a recipe," she told us many times, "if you don't understand how all of the ingredients need to come together. A diagram of a sentence shows you where everything needs to go, all in the right portions." Subjects, predicates, direct and indirect objects, prepositions, modifiers, articles, dependent clauses (so difficult to identify!) and the great connectors, the conjunctions, were all diagrammed with patience and a dash of creativity, always starting with a horizontal line, then divided by a series of vertical lines. A vertical dividing line always had the subject located with certainty to its left, the verb was usually situated equitably and reliably in the middle, the modifiers hanging like adventurers by their fingertips off diagonal lines below the word they were modifying. "And here is our modifier!" Mrs. Williams would exclaim, her voice happy, turning from the blackboard to all of us, her face beaming. "Here she is!" Years later, when I became a sportswriter and had occasion to spend a lot of time with high school and college coaches in their offices, the coaches would sometimes diagram their plays in order to give me better insight into what they were doing. I almost always would think of Mrs. Williams' sentence diagramming. The best coaches, no matter the sport, were just like Mrs. Williams in that respect. They would diagram their plays in a clear, confident, and completely legible hand, drawing with an enthused and invested care, like a family member creating a brief genealogy. These were championship-caliber coaches. And I could see Mrs. Williams' rapt attention to detail, her deep respect for the fundamentals, and her reverence for anyone who could find the joy in these most basic but necessary of tasks in every one of them.

We were taught these basics in what for me felt like the most thrilling manner possible. And in addition to learning the basics, Mrs. Williams encouraged us to read the classics—classics for the sixth-grade mind, of course. *Call of the Wild* by Jack London. *Black Beauty* by Anna Sewell. *My Side of the Mountain* by Jean Craighead George. As we read, Mrs. Williams also asked us to write. We would write "themes" (Mrs. Williams never called them book reports) about the books we had read, with Mrs. Williams encouraging us to not just re-tell the plot but go a little deeper into our thoughts and emotions. Mrs. Williams always offered praise for my themes. She began asking me how many books, and what kind of books, I read at home. When I told her that my favorite magazine was "The Sporting News," she smiled knowingly. "All you boys love your baseball box scores, don't you?" she said, sounding more like a mom who had a son of her own than a teacher. When I told her I wished I could check more books out of the Stead Elementary School library, she had a solution for me: Why not get a Washoe County Library card? Problem was, I didn't know exactly how to do that. One day not long after our conversation, Mrs. Williams made a special trip of her own to the palatial downtown Reno Washoe County Library. She gathered some materials, including a form on how to get a library card, and brought them to school for me so I could get my own Washoe County Library card.

It was during this time that Mrs. Williams, not for all lunch hours, but at least a couple of times a week, allowed me to stay inside her classroom to write. We were progressing from the basics of grammar and sentence diagramming to themes to creative writing. I was beginning to really enjoy the process of writing. I could fill a page quickly, but what hooked me was the re-reading, the editing, and the re-writing that would often help polish and make simpler what I was trying to say. My stories were adventure stories, inspired by the Jack London we read in class and the *Mutiny on the Bounty* authors Nordhoff and Hall, the first book I ever checked out from the Stead Branch of the Washoe County Library with my brand-new library card. Mrs. Williams and Mr. Williams, during the times when they shared their lunch hours at her desk, every so often would ask, "You're doing OK, John?" and I would quickly reply, with a distracted nod, "I'm doing fine, thank you," quickly turning back to my scribbling down of some sort of high-seas drama set in the 18th century or a wildland adventure set in late 19th or 20th century Alaska. I remember one lunch hour sitting at my desk and hearing Mr. Williams exclaim in his Oklahoma drawl, "My oh my, Shineesta, that boy of yours sure loves to write!" The room was dead quiet, and then I accidentally dropped my pencil to the floor. I snatched the pencil up frantically, like a church-goer who had just dropped communion and got right back to my writing. "See," Mr. Williams added, "nothing is going to stop John from his writing!" And then the three of us couldn't help it. We all but burst out into laughter. When it came time for the class to share its creative work, Mrs. Williams read many of the pieces aloud to us. I will always remember what she said to our class about my story: "John feels things very deeply. Whenever you read something that John has written, you also feel things very deeply, too. He has a great gift."

I was extremely lucky to be in Mrs. Williams' sixth grade class at Stead Elementary. She encouraged me at an age where just the slightest bit of positive reinforcement can have a profound impact on a young person's life. She was one of the first people to ever tell me I could be good at something. The fact that she often went out of her way to do this has always made me aspire to do the same with the people I've come to know in my life. To be like Mrs. Shineesta Williams was to see the good in all people, and to try to help them realize their best talents in the most constructive and loving manner possible. It was an honor to be her student. Mrs. Williams passed away in 1991. Mr. Williams passed away in 2012.

Finding Running, and Myself

Coach Lyle Freeman wasn't my first coach if you happen to count various T-Ball, Little League, Babe Ruth, and youth basketball coaches I had while I was growing up. But to this day, I think of him as my only true, official coach. For the better part of five years, from eighth grade and culminating with my senior year of high school, Coach Freeman was a constant presence in my life.

I took up running during the summer of 1976, inspired by watching Olympic Marathon champion Frank Shorter come up just short, finishing second at the Montreal Olympics in his bid to become the first person to ever win consecutive Olympic Marathon titles. Watching Shorter on TV as he fought gamely on the rainy streets of Montreal, chasing after East Germany's Waldemar Cierpinski (who it later turned out was implicated in East Germany's systematic doping system of its Olympic athletes), left a life-altering impression on me. I was struck by how fluid Shorter's running was. How his face, deeply angled with concentration, could also convey the look of a person who felt liberated, free to think about whatever they wished. And, most remarkably to a 13-year-old who couldn't yet fathom running such long distances, how it also seemed that Frank Shorter was running as fast as he humanly could for the entirety of 26.2 miles, and how the roads of Montreal, when confronted with such a perfect combination of focus and personal passion, had no choice but to be absorbed directly into that person's entire being.

I began running around our neighborhood not long after. We had moved from Stead into Reno the year before. At first, my running that August was frustrating. I would start too quickly and just as quickly grow fatigued, having to walk back to our home on Plumb Lane in Reno. I had no idea what I was doing. I wore "gym shoes," the Chuck Taylor Converse All-Stars that I had worn in P.E. class during my seventh-grade year. My parents took me to the Sportsman sporting goods store in downtown Reno and bought me a small silver-colored stopwatch that I would click on at the start of every one-mile run, then click off when I had finished. By the time the school year started at Darrell C. Swope Middle School a few weeks later, I knew I wanted to go out for the cross-country team, led by Coach Freeman.

Coach Freeman was in his late 20s then. He was not far removed from his collegiate athletic career at the University of Nevada in Reno, where he had competed on the gymnastics team. He was an incredibly fit individual. As you'd be driven to school by your parents, you'd often see Coach Freeman running to school from his tidy little home on

Gear Street, located not far from the university campus. There would be a light backpack with his school clothes inside swinging contentedly back and forth on his bony shoulders. His pace was always steady and strong, not belying the fact that his home on Gear Street was probably a good four miles from Swope. None of us ever added his mileage up then, but looking back now, in a typical day in addition to teaching six periods of physical education classes, coaching (and running with) the cross-country team after school, slinging his backpack on his shoulders, and then running home, Coach Freeman was easily putting in around 10 to 12 miles of running each day. There could be snow on the ground in the winter or there could be fierce winds blowing off the Sierra in the spring, and it wouldn't matter. It seemed as if Coach Freeman was always running. Coach Freeman was the first person I'd ever been around who not only ran, but who *lived* as a runner.

My running improved dramatically under Coach Freeman's tutelage. I was never a champion, never much more than an average middle school and high school runner. But thanks to Coach Freeman's optimistic nature, his encouragement, and his creative and unorthodox coaching methods, I learned how to be a runner. He had a coaching philosophy that was grounded in the crucible of hard work. He believed that the only way a young runner could overcome any personal doubts or demons about the prospect of running long distances was by challenging themselves to do just that—run long distances. Not so much in middle school, but definitely in high school, our workouts under Coach Freeman were long, arduous affairs that sometimes took hours to complete. Spring break in high school wasn't a vacation for us. Spring break meant double days. Meeting as a team to run for five miles before any of us had even eaten breakfast, then meeting again in the afternoon for speed workouts where we would run 20, 30, or even 40 400-meter timed repeats or punishing 10-mile runs on the roads.

Coach Freeman tempered the intensity, pain, and duration of the workouts with fun interludes that felt quirky and appealed to the fun-and-games nature of teens. He'd have us do some of the most off-the-wall workouts imaginable. It was a free-flowing form of cross training before anyone had ever coined the term. Like grabbing a medicine ball and sprinting as fast as we could with it around the Reno High School track. Or ending the week on Friday, the day before a meet, with a game of team handball, a game none of us had ever heard of but Coach Freeman had seen and fallen in love with when he had traveled to Germany in 1972 to spectate at the Summer Olympic Games in Munich. You'd run madly up and down the field, passing, dribbling, or hitting a small rubber ball (never kicking it) and eventually trying to throw the ball into a guarded goal. An hour would pass by without you realizing you had been running and sprinting for an hour straight. Or there would be days during cross country season when Coach Freeman would have us jog over to the softball fields of nearby Idlewild Park. While Coach Freeman would position himself in the middle of the fields, a coach's whistle hanging from his mouth, we would take our shoes and socks off, and then run barefoot on the grass. The soft thrill of the grass made whatever was clouding our young high school minds dissolve instantly. Then after waiting for a few minutes as our minds idled and our feet danced playfully over the grass, Coach Freeman would blow his whistle. Like Pavlov's dog, we were all conditioned that when you heard Coach Freeman's whistle, it was your do-or-die duty to sprint along the outfield of the softball field as fast as you possibly could. Not until you heard the next whistle, which could be in 15 seconds or could drag on terribly for two or three minutes, would you be allowed to slow to a jog. And then, before you had completely recovered, your chest heaving uncontrollably in and out, there would be another whistle breaking the peace of the fall afternoon air—another order to challenge yourself to charge across the grass yet again. Only Coach Freeman knew how long the whistle blasts would be and how long the workout would last. It taught us to learn how to shift gears, to expect the unexpected in any race that we ran. We came from these experiences to instinctively understand that all races could never be scripted ahead of time. There would be welcomed ebbs and unexpected painful flows that would pull us along with the force of a flood. We learned from Coach Freeman that it was up to us, individually, to rise up and convince ourselves that we were capable and had the capacity to find ways to run through the challenge of growing and, eventually, unrelenting pain in order to get to the finish. To this day, whenever I find myself accelerating into a turn on a trail, whether in training or in a race, I think of Coach Freeman blowing his whistle, surprising us, testing us, convincing us that we had at least one more surge of defiance left in our legs.

Coach Freeman also provided quiet counsel, sometimes in words, but often through actions that spoke more loudly than his words. He smiled often and laughed just as often as he smiled. His laugh sounded like a machine gun; it came at you in one long burst of ha-ha-ha-ha-ha-ha-ha that sprayed you, completely covering you with its enthusiasm. I don't recall him ever losing his temper, or even so much as raising his voice in disappointment or discouragement with us. He was fond of using the word "day." Every day was special. Before our races, he would smile with extreme confidence in all of us and tell us to "have a day." If we ran well, we "had a day!" If we didn't run well or perform up to expectations, there would always be "another day." Now that I run ultra marathons, which sometimes (quite often now that I'm older) can start one day and finish late in the next, I find it interesting that my high school coach measured the value of everything that we did in those same terms. An accomplishment wasn't an accomplishment unless it was measured in a succession of days of practice and training, an accumulation of days paid in preparation and honoring the process, the price you paid in sacrifice, for "having a day."

What made Coach Freeman so fun to be around was how clearly aware he was of the absurd lengths we would all often go to in order to get in a workout or push ourselves beyond what was expected. "Anything that is worth it, no matter what it is," he often told us, "is worth giving it all you have." Because of this philosophy, he never missed a workout. He expected us to do the same. We ran no matter the conditions. Coach Freeman always seemed most proud of us when the weather was terrible and we had raced or gotten through one of his epic workouts. Springtime in Reno can be particularly brutal, with afternoon winds that can swoop into our valley with a demonic force. Spring track season often felt like you were precariously perched on a crag in the Himalayas, the harsh wind violently whipping your clothing against skin that felt like it wanted to whimper. There was an 800-meter race I ran on one of those days, on a gray cinder track at a neighboring high school, and I actually broke free of the field with about 200 meters to go, on my way to one of the few wins I'd ever experience in high school. I can still see Coach Freeman sprinting across the infield to meet me as I raced to the finish line, the white ski cap flying off of his head, the thermal of wind lifting it like a balloon into the air, his arms pumping wildly. Coach Freeman wasn't a hugger, but he hugged me that day, proud not only that I had won but that I had given it my all in such terrible, bone-chilling, lung-burning conditions.

Since my running career didn't have many wins like the one I had on that windy day, I came to realize that Coach Freeman had different expectations for his different runners. We were both Pisces, known for our sensitive souls, and we even shared the same birthday on February 20. Perhaps he could see a little of himself in how I wasn't afraid to go all-in and never miss a workout or a practice. But it was more than that. Coach Freeman was a great coach because he never thought of his athletes as one-dimensional figures. We weren't flat cut-outs to him. We were all full of nuance and varying motivations. Coach Freeman's approach with me was more about keeping me running, exhorting me to keep going. One time I grew so frustrated with my running that I tossed my green Nike Waffle Racers onto the roof of our school. A few days later, on one of the weekend runs we'd have from Coach Freeman's little bungalow on Gear Street, the Waffle Racers were sitting on his front porch, patiently waiting for me. I asked him how long they'd taken up residence on his porch. "Oh, a couple of days," he smiled. "But at least they're a pair. At least they have company."

After I'd failed to qualify for the state championships during our regional meet of my senior track season, on an infernally hot day on the dirt track at Douglas High School, I grabbed my sweats with tears in my eyes and ran under the bleachers as my head pounded from delirium, dehydration, and disappointment. Coach Freeman sought me out, nearly hitting his head on the low-hanging metal. His message to me was a simple one. "You have nothing to be ashamed of. We'll see you next week for some runs, JT," he said. My high school running career was over. But my running wasn't. Coach Freeman had seen to that. More than 40 years later, I am still a runner. If not for Coach Freeman, who always saw me as a runner and who always instinctively knew that inside of me was always a yearning to go on another run, I kept going. Somehow, he knew that somewhere down the road, as long as I kept going and didn't quit running, there was something special awaiting me. I wonder if my life would've been the running life that it has been if not for Coach Freeman. I had wanted to disappear beneath the bleachers of Douglas High School and not be seen again and probably not ever run again. He wasn't about to let me get away with that. Through the special, indispensable elation and energy that Coach Freeman put into running, I learned how to run. But it was through his eyes that saw me for what I was, not a potential champion or even a middle-of-the-pack competitor, but as a person who had become enlivened and had discovered something intensely personal, meaningful, and worth doing. I had become a runner.

Today, Coach Freeman is in his 70s. He's retired now, after a distinguished high school coaching career that saw his teams and athletes win dozens of Nevada state championships in cross country and track. He doesn't live very far from that Douglas High School track and those bleachers I tried to hide beneath in shame more than 40 years ago. He promised me then that we'd go on some runs and that my head would clear from the throbbing sorrow of that day and my sadness would dissipate and things would get better. Coach Freeman was never wrong. He knew that all days are precious and worth wanting to "have a day." More than that, though, he knew the value of always striving and seeking, of always wanting to run "another day."

In Mrs. Williams and Coach Freeman I had found two people who saw something special in me. I doubt very seriously that their interest in me was in the hopes of developing the next Pulitzer Prize-winning writer or coaching the next Olympic champion runner. My abilities are far more modest than that. No, their interest and encouragement were rooted more in helping a young person recognize they were capable of doing so much more. As I grew into young adulthood, into my college years and beyond, I began to realize that I loved writing and running with an equal fervor. It was hard to do one without thinking of the other. Whenever I was out on long runs or in a race, I would find myself often floating above the effort, almost as if in a sweat-filled, oxygen-deprived dream. And from that heightened altitude where I was as much an observer as a participant, I'd come to see the long run or the race in terms of a story unfolding before me—a story that I might one day tell. There was always a beginning, a middle, and an end to every race. There were always incredible dramatic arcs filled with heroic acts from the heroines and heroes that I shared the roads and the trails with. Sometimes, as in a story, the ending would be indeterminate. I'd finish a race, but what did it mean in the big picture? Had I grown as a runner? As a person? Had I learned or experienced anything worth saving and carrying with me throughout my life? As I've grown older, the expectations for my running have matured as well. Whenever I finish a race today, the first thought after the pain and stiffness has muted, always focuses on self-awareness and self-actualization: Is there anything that I've just experienced that can help me become a better person?

All of this creates a common vocabulary of experience. Runners often share the same running dreams, and whenever I speak, I speak as one of them. I feel I've always been able to speak more easily to runners because of my background as a writer and a journalist, which inevitably steers me into a mode of assembling facts and then inferring a greater and more universal meaning. I remember an interview I conducted more than 30 years ago with a runner named Ralph Pidcock in a small diner here in Reno. Ralph was in his 60s then. He was balding, wasn't particularly fast, and had a sly sense of humor. He was a social worker at the local V.A. Hospital and made it a point to run the same route every day from his small apartment on the west side of Reno, up North Virginia Street past the University of Nevada, Reno campus, to the small Bonanza Casino diner. Ralph would walk right into the diner still in his running clothes, find himself a nice booth, order a cup of coffee, talk to the servers, read the newspaper for a while, then run back home. He did this often before the sun came up and before his work at the V.A. would begin. Ralph said his nickname, "Goldfinger," a nod to the 1964 spy film of the same name, was actually based on the yellow shorts and yellow race singlet he always wore. "Everything I touch in running turns to gold," Ralph said with an impish wink. Ralph was a warm and welcoming person. After I wrote an article about him and his daily ritual—one he repeated for many years without fail—a number of people from throughout the country, particularly from Indiana and Ohio, wrote me letters mentioning they had come to know Ralph when he had been part of their running communities earlier in his life. (Included in the correspondence about Ralph was a letter from the legendary *Runner's World* columnist and editor, Hal Higdon, a runner and writer I've always greatly admired, who fondly recalled Ralph for his punctuality and his passion for the sport). At one point during our interview, Ralph wondered why I found runners so interesting. "Because no matter who they are, they have something heroic inside of them," I said, surprising myself with how dramatic my response sounded. Ralph took a long swig from his coffee. He smiled. Goldfinger knew exactly what I was talking about. Goldfinger was someone known throughout the Midwest, as well as now, in his new community in Northern Nevada. *There really is a hero in all runners*, Ralph's knowing smile seemed to be saying. "You sound like a typical writer," he said. "And you sound like what every runner would hope to be."

From my childhood with Mrs. Williams and Coach Freeman to who I am today, it is hard to tell where the writer ends and the runner begins inside of me. I'm glad that the two are never far removed from one another, whether it is in the middle of the night at an aid station (where I am surrounded by equally exhausted ultra runners who are sensing their dreams are either slowly drifting away or are magically coming back to life), or when I'm writing about running and runners, amazed by the sheer physical imperatives of the distances we run and how our time in these lonely places also reaffirms in us once we've finished a deep desire to be part of something larger than ourselves.

Running and writing are probably two of the most solitary endeavors. Yet they are, at their core, both inherently about connection. In ultra running, it is about finding kindred spirits who share the same desire to conquer remarkably long distances. Whenever I run across a first-time ultra runner, I always make it a point to remind them that in ultra running, you are never alone and are usually quite lucky to have so many people around you who are just as invested as you are in going the distance. In writing, it is about finding an audience, and a larger community as well, to share stories and exchange ideas. A book group isn't all that dissimilar from a training group. There are usually good stores to share, decent food and drink to consume, and friendships to make that can last a lifetime. I've been lucky to have paired running and writing throughout my life. They've both come to help me share, to reach out, and to become part of a larger group of people. My running reminds me it's not uncommon at all to have gone through something so remarkably similar with so many other runners. And it is my writing that always reminds me to take a step back for a moment, to let my mind wander, to rise above the race, and to see things from an altitude of wonder, realizing how these efforts always mirror the human condition and how remarkable it is to have run these great distances in the first place.

CHAPTER 2

A Fall, a Rescue, and
a Changed Life

Western States was being cruel to me, and with each blow the race delivered, I was getting closer to reaching my emotional and physical breaking point. It hadn't started out that way, of course. My 1995 pacing duties with Joe had been absolute magic. It only made sense that I should try running the race myself. Joe's 10th-place finish at age 51, outrunning a couple of amazing Tarahumara runners, had made it all look too easy. I found that out the hard way during my own Western States run in 1997. I ran completely focused on and thoroughly mesmerized by nothing but the shiniest of all objects in ultra running— the coveted sub-24-hour Western States silver belt buckle. Over the next few years, I kept coming back, or tried to come back to, Western States. Each experience seemed to grow progressively worse and more self-defeating. I've often wondered why this was so. Why did Western States still hold my imagination the way it did? And why did I want to keep coming back to it, even as I seemingly moved farther away from, rather than achieving, my goal of having the kind of special run that Joe had enjoyed in 1995? A little history is in order here, first to explain the origins of Western States, how it grew in popularity, how it hooked me in the late 1990s, how it nearly broke me not long after, and how a chance meeting in the "high country" portion of the course in 2000 changed everything for me.

Welcome to Western States

Western States began in 1974 as part of the 20th edition of the One Hundred Miles in One Day Western States Trail Ride (also known as the "Tevis Cup"), from Olympic Valley, California on Lake Tahoe's north shore to Auburn. Twenty-seven-year-old Harry "Gordy" Ainsleigh, a local woodcutter, was planning to run, rather than ride, the entire distance. Gordy, who had grown up near Auburn in Colfax, California, was a strong endurance athlete. He was well over 6 feet tall and weighed 205 pounds. The *Auburn Journal* in July 1974 described him as a "strapping" distance runner. For those of us who have run with Gordy, the word "agile" also comes to mind. During the 1990s, when I came of age in ultra running, there were many times during races when I would slow as I approached a fallen log or a tricky rock outcropping that required some care in order to maneuver around it. I'd think too much. I would slow to weigh the possibilities of what to do. And then the 50-ish-year-old Gordy would run right past me. He was a much more intuitive and confident runner and person. He wouldn't even break stride. He'd hurdle the fallen log or sidestep the rocky outcropping with a quick flick of his hips that made him look like a dancer doing a tango. A sure-footed hop or two later, and then Gordy would be gone, steamrolling his way up the trail. I still remember my 1997 run at Western States, how I knew I was on the razor's edge of making the finish in under 24 hours. Right out of the Auburn Lakes Trail aid station near mile 85, in the dark of a night that wasn't made any easier because of the failing batteries in my flashlight, Gordy swooped by me like the trail was illuminated with the blinding mid-day sun. He looked like a confident NFL running back who had just powered through a couple of irritating tacklers, speeding through the darkness with total and expert control. He was dictating to the trail how this finish was going to play out. He wasn't about to let the trail deter him in any way. I ran more reactively, fearfully, and let the trail slow me. I missed a silver belt buckle and 24 hours by 96 seconds. Gordy ran as a person whose intimate trail knowledge and inner belief in himself was guiding him to the finish he wanted. He finished in 23:38.

Gordy's effort in 1974 remains one of the great tales in ultra running. He was following in the footsteps of seven U.S. Army infantry soldiers who in 1972 had successfully hiked the ride course, finishing in times that ranged from 44 to 46 hours. In 1974, Gordy was vying to become the first person to run the ride course in under the allotted event time limit of 24 hours. It is instructive today to think of Gordy's run not so much as history-making, nor as the creation of 100-mile trail running in North America, but simply as a compelling story of human endurance in the face of daunting odds. In interviews and in the conversations Gordy has had with trail friends over the years, the basic details surrounding the events of August 3-4, 1974, for the most part have remained some-what the same. To begin with, the odds were definitely not in Gordy's favor as he planned his run with the horses during the 20th edition of the One Hundred Miles in One Day Western States Trail Ride. In fact, the co-founder of the Western States Trail Ride, Wendell T. Robie, who was friends with Gordy, didn't think Gordy would make it. A few days before the event, in late July, Robie told the *Auburn Journal*, "It is probably a universal opinion that it is beyond the powers of human endurance to span the 100 miles of this rough mountainous trail on foot in a period of 24 hours (the horse ride had an absolute cutoff of 24 hours for all finishers), but Harry will probably make one or two of the control (aid) stations within the operational schedule provided for the inspection of horses. At least we pray to God he does."

Like all good stories, you had to love the personal contrasts between Gordy, with his mane of long, blonde hair and full beard that made him look more like a handsome, mysterious lead guitarist of an early 1970s rock band, and white-haired, stern-faced Robie, whose love of the surrounding mountains was a driving current throughout his life. Robie felt the mountains' mere presence was a beckoning to people's souls to go out and experience them, from the Sierra and the snow-covered peaks in and around Donner Summit (which through Robie's promotion in the 1930s, marked the beginning of the modern California ski industry) all the way down through the stunning ridgelines above the drainages of the wild waters of the American River. Both Gordy and Robie, though they possessed different temperaments, were explorers and adventurers at heart. If somehow Gordy were to finish before the allotted time of 24 hours had expired, there was no doubt that Wendell Robie (who even in his 70s was also still competing in the Tevis Cup himself and would finish that year's event in 29th place) was among those rooting with all their heart for Gordy to go the distance.

The first Lake Tahoe-to-Auburn trail ride was held on August 7, 1955, when Robie and three other riders successfully completed the trek from Tahoe City to Auburn in under 24 hours. By 1974, there were 237 people from around the country riding in the event. Anything that Wendell Robie did was worthy of major headlines in the area. Born in Auburn, he could trace his family's roots back to some of the earliest discoveries of gold in California at nearby Gold Run. He was a former Placer High School student body president, and his Auburn Lumber

Company and Heart Federal Savings and Loan were pillars of the community. The *Auburn Journal* once wrote of Robie, "It would have been difficult for any resident of Auburn not to have known and met Wendell Robie." Appetite for news about the Western States Trail Ride was such that there were live reports on a local radio station, K-POP 1110 AM radio, provided by the popular radio personality Gene Ragle throughout the weekend. Although the event might have seemed small to the outside world, for the radius connecting Olympic Valley to Auburn that weekend in 1974, there was an electric sense of anticipation and excitement. Robie told the *Auburn Journal* that the 1974 ride, with Gordy running with the horses, would "be a little different" than in years past.

Although he was alone when he left the starting line about 15 minutes before the ride began, there was a lot riding on Gordy's shoulders on the morning of August 3, 1974. He soon realized that being on foot was extremely challenging—not because of facing the unknown, but because of the disruptive reality he faced as the field of horse riders began catching up to him on the trail. Gordy was soon running in fast and physically taxing intervals. He'd have to pick up his pace to a fast run to keep his place on the single-track trail and stay ahead of some of the horses, who were moving at a fast race trot. Inevitably the horses would catch him, and Gordy would have to move to the side of the trail, letting a few of the riders pass before more horses caught up with him. The day was also hot. In interviews, Gordy has said the temperatures that day rose to 107 degrees. National Weather Service data indicate that the high that day in Auburn was 92 degrees, still hot enough. By the time Gordy reached the Devil's Thumb medical checkpoint, which was a little before halfway and came after a tortuous near 2,000-foot climb in a little less than two miles up a series of steep, unrelenting switchbacks, he was convinced that he was done. Luckily, two of his friends took him into the shade of the pines, gave him water and salt tablets, and massaged his legs. About a half hour later, Gordy was revived. He ran the rest of the way with a simple goal in mind. As long as he maintained the ability to take at least one more step forward, no matter the terrain, no matter the heat, no matter the fatigue, Gordy felt he was going to get to the finish line in Auburn.

And he did. Gordy finished in 23:42. The *Auburn Journal* reported that as Gordy crossed the finish line in Auburn, such an "exhausting feat" had "nevertheless failed to impair his ability to turn a few cartwheels and perform some headstands after he trotted into McCann Stadium."

Gordy's run inspired other runners to run with the horses. In 1975, another local runner, Ron Kelley, attempted to duplicate Gordy's feat. He dropped out with two miles remaining. In 1976, one of the true characters of Sierra Nevada endurance sports history, Ken "Cowman" Shirk, who ran with a set of cow horns on his head, successfully completed the route, though about 30 minutes past the 24-hour ride time limit. By 1977, a separate running event, the Western States Endurance Run, was held. Fourteen runners started. Three finished, with Andy Gonzales the only one finishing in under 24 hours, in 22:57. Since then, the Western States Endurance Run has only grown in renown and popularity. In December 2022, there were more than 7,000 runners from throughout the world entered in the Western States lottery, hoping to earn one of the 369 spots that are available each year.

Stepping Into History

As I began to run the race myself in 1997, all of this history held a tight grip on me. Some of it was still alive, like seeing the kind, caring, and distinguished face of Dr. Robert Lind, who was on hand in 1977 for the first official running of Western States to monitor the health of the 14 runners that day. Dr. Lind would go on to serve as the event's medical director for the next three decades. Or, meeting two of the most important female figures in the history of the race, longtime board members Mo Livermore and Shannon Weil, who both were encouraged in the late 1970s by Robie to help organize the Western States run. Mo and Shannon helped give the event its soul and its distinctive can-do positive energy, what some affectionately called "Mo-Shan." Or, coming to share the Western States Trail in the late 1990s with runners who even then had long histories with the event and who spoke of its majesty, challenge, and ability to change one's life forever in the most reverential of terms. I was hooked. I came to view Western States as the most important running challenge I'd ever encountered in my life.

The 1997 race was a 100-mile accomplishment tainted by a 96-second disappointment. I expected redemption and the silver belt buckle in 1998 but found more disappointment instead. I wrenched my knee on the snow and ice of the high country in the early portions of the race and could never work through the pain. I dropped at the Rucky Chucky river crossing at mile 78. In 1999, the Western States lottery gods didn't smile on me. I wasn't chosen that year. I gained entry again in 2000. I was strong and fit that year. By some stroke of luck, I had actually thrived on the snow that had enveloped the nearby Carson Range, a sharp-edged range of mountains hugging Reno's west flank, and won our local 50-miler, Silver State, that May. Not long after that win, I'd received an email from five-time Western States champion Tim Twietmeyer. It read in part, "I have no doubt by the time this year's race is over, you'll be wearing silver."

Oh, You Can Go On

Everything on the morning of June 24, 2000 started smoothly. A slight low-pressure system had moved in the day before. There was a pleasant breeze in Olympic Valley on Friday as the runners had checked in for Saturday's race. Race day would hit "only" 89 degrees. The high country had scant evidence of the epic covering of snow that had lasted more than 25 miles two years before. A little before the 16-mile mark and the Red Star Ridge aid station, I was moving easily, enjoying the view of one of Western States' many amazing ridgelines, where the mountains of Tahoe were still visible behind us, with the nearby headwaters of the American River having carved out the looming lonely volcanic-colored landscape that would soon be challenging us. It was pure wonder as I made way along that ridgeline, the miles coming too easily.

And then the reverie I was experiencing shattered. I tripped on a root that was slyly obscured in the dust of the trail. I went down hard, a shrill cry of surprise leaving my lips. I landed on both of my knees, feeling the skin tear and burn instantly from the dirt and rock, and did a half-roll onto my side. A puff of stale trail dust enveloped me, and I remember looking at it and thinking that it looked like exhaust from a car that had just backfired and then stalled out. Whether the dust really did resemble smoke didn't matter. It rose lazily into the air, and with both my knees burning with pain, I felt utterly helpless to even stand up, let alone continue on with the race. My dreams of running Western States the way I had always hoped seemed to condense right into the air, like that ocher dust rising above me.

My past history with Western States immediately ran through my mind. Crying in 1997 at the finish line when I had come up 96 seconds short. Limping off the course at mile 78 in 1998. Sitting at home and completely missing the event in 1999. And now, being knocked to the ground in 2000. Western States was being too cruel to me.

I can't remember now. I either said the following, or at the very least thought it:

"Goddammit! What the fuck else can happen to me?"

Then I felt some hands on my back. Before I had a chance to respond, I could feel the hands very gently, but firmly, grip underneath my armpits, pulling me to my feet. A man I could immediately tell was older than I was, with blond hair and the most striking blue eyes I'd ever seen, smiled at me.

"Are you OK?" he asked. His grin was expansive, full of big white teeth, a physical manifestation of the way this person, I would come to discover, always was. Scotty Mills was a smiler, a doer, and a person who was never overwhelmed by any challenge. As I stood next to him, my knees bloodied and my mind a little woozy from my fall, I was struck by his permanence. He wore the standard-issue ultra "uniform" that so many of us white, early-middle-aged to middle-aged runners wore in the late 1990s and early 2000s—white hat and white shirt to deflect the scorching and draining rays of the sun and black running shorts. But unlike so many of us, who wore the outfit in a quiet, let-me-blend-in-to-the-background kind of way, it was how Scotty's black shorts were practically plastered to his muscular legs that caught my attention. His legs were like tree trunks, as dominant as I'd ever seen, a product of having played collegiate soccer at the Air Force Academy. They were so firm and permanent looking, it was hard to imagine them being vulnerable to any type of injury. Maybe the only thing they would be susceptible to was some kind tree disease like oak wilt or cedar rust. Scotty's inner confidence and physical sturdiness steadied me almost immediately. His smile made me smile, though there were still dark thoughts racing through my head.

"I don't know if I'm OK," I said. "I really don't know if I want to go on."

"Oh, you can go on," he said. "I'll tell you what. Let's just run on a little bit, together, and see how things go. I think you're going to be all right."

I nodded. We started to run. Scotty introduced himself. I told him who I was. Scotty patiently let me explain my story. He said he could relate to some of my disappointment. I discovered that he had been an ultra runner for a long time, and that he carried his many races around with him, good and bad, and that they all resonated with him in a very deep way. Their meaning was the way memory was for most people—how we feel a glow of reassurance when they are good, how we can become obsessively haunted by them when they are bad, and how in their passing transience there is (in Scotty's case at least) a patience and understanding in how we come to view ourselves. Scotty was 49 years old, and he identified as many things: a husband, a friend, a graduate of the Air Force Academy, and an Air Force officer. But he had been a runner for a long time, and all of his many races, including his first finish at Western States some 18 years earlier in 1982, had come to define him as well. He seemed perfectly OK with this fact. Running was permanently his. And perhaps out of all the things that we do in life, it might've been the one thing that Scotty was determined to do for all of his days.

We ran together that day for more than 60 miles. I don't know if I will ever run a more important 60 miles in my life. There are times when you just happen to find a shared rhythm and purpose with the person you are running with, and that was what came to characterize our day together. Scotty was hoping to break 20 hours that day, but he backed off his time goal—a time goal he had always cherished, having come excruciatingly close on a couple of occasions, including in 1991 when he missed breaking 20 hours by a mere three seconds in order to help me. Most runners might've made sure I was upright, maybe a few might've also helped to wipe off the blood. But then they would have left me. Not Scotty. I had only one Western States finish under my belt. Scotty at that point was shooting for Western States finish No. 8.

He made sure I got cleaned off by the volunteers when we ran into the Red Star Ridge aid station a mile or so after we'd first met. "It's always important that you feel fresh," Scotty said as one of the volunteers wiped the blood off my knees. "Even if you get tired 80 miles into a race, it doesn't mean that you still can't feel fresh and feel good about what you're doing."

Wise Companions Are Forged in Experience

Scotty had been a Navigator Training Officer, and like any good teacher, he dropped gentle bits of advice on me throughout the day. Don't be afraid to walk up the hills instead of charge up them. Always keep the bandana around your neck wet to take the sting off the heat. Make sure you walk, don't run, out of the aid stations so you can properly finish eating and drinking. Don't be in such a hurry that you forget to take care of the essentials and forget something important. Take care to think of fueling and drinking throughout the 100-mile distance not like you were a college kid in a chug-a-thon where copious amounts are consumed in one gut-busting bender, but rather try to emulate the more therapeutic, deliberate, and steady flow of an IV-drip. Nothing to the extreme, but in regular intervals where you can find a pleasing stasis, so that you were never lacking food, drink, or energy. I came to discover that Scotty wasn't just a lone wolf runner, out only for himself. He was a runner of substance, a person of sincere feeling, who felt an abiding need to share and to give back. Scotty was a run organizer, a race director and, when it was all said and done, a connector of people. Scotty was living at the time in Virginia with his wife, Jean, who had also been an Air Force officer. He was an integral part of what was known as the Virginia Happy Trails Running Club, a group of friendly trail runners who were popularizing the sport on the eastern seaboard. Since 1996, he'd been the race director of one of the East's classic "old-school" ultras, the Bull Run 50, which was run on the famed Civil War battle-ground of the same name.

As the years passed, Scotty eventually retired from the Air Force. By 2007, he and Jean had relocated to the San Diego area. He became immersed in the ultra community there. He joined the San Diego Ultra Running Friends (SURF) group. He began race directing one of the area's crown jewel events, the San Diego hundred-miler in the nearby stark-yet-beautiful Laguna Mountains, a longtime spring and summer-time springboard of dreams for the through-hikers of the Pacific Crest Trail.

As our friendship grew, what impressed me most about Scotty was as he grew older, still running and finishing the country's most challenging races like the Hardrock 100 and Western States well into his 60s, his number of friends continued to grow. His life had been in direct contrast to how we are supposed to age in this country. We grow so accustomed to the sad reality that often as we age, the possibilities of our world begin to shrink substantially. As we get older, the inevitable rite of passage is, we have to consider giving things up and not adding anything to our lives. Each year past our retirement age often becomes a slow, dispiriting, and lonely slog to the rest home. Not so with Scotty. He was a regular presence at all SURF events like the annual New Year's Day "Fat-Ass" (meaning an untimed, utterly uncompetitive, and only lightly organized gathering) run where racing and training plans would be hatched for the coming year. Scotty made friends easily because he was always such an encouraging presence, no matter what a person's age, background, or gender was. The comparison might sound odd, but I've always thought about Scotty in the same way I think about former President Jimmy Carter's mother, Lillian. For those who don't remem-ber Miss Lillian, she was a woman before her time. She disagreed with the segregated ways of the southern state she grew up in and often stood up against them. She was a person who was constantly eager to learn new things, and in her 60s, she volunteered and served in the Peace Corps for 21 months in India. She believed throughout her life that it is every human being's duty to be of service to others. I've seen all of these same attributes in a muscular, retired Air Force officer who not only asks a lot of himself, but who expects others to see the value of volunteering, of helping, of being not only of support, but of substance.

Scotty's relationship with his good friend and trail running buddy Angela Shartel is a good example of how he makes a difference in the lives of those he knows. There is a 22-year age difference between the two of them, and in some ways their relationship feels like one that would exist between a father and a daughter. Angela was a mother of three. In the years following the birth of her children, she struggled with numerous issues, including postpartum depression, weight gain, borderline diabetes, and the end of her first marriage. She was on medication for depression, anxiety, and high blood pressure. She turned to a more active lifestyle, including weight training and running. She ran road races and marathons. By 2008, Angela was running ultra marathons. Her first real interaction with Scotty started in a shaky fashion. He was race-directing another San Diego ultra mainstay, the Noble Canyon 50K. Angela missed the registration deadline. She called Scotty and begged her way in. Then she forgot that the race was on a Saturday. She showed up the next day, on a Sunday, and nobody was there. Embarrassed and contrite, Angela offered to still pay Scotty the entry fee for the spot in the race he had promised her. Scotty told Angela no, that wouldn't be necessary. The two began running together instead. They've been close friends ever since. Over the past decade, whenever Angela has run an important race, usually Scotty and her other close trail running friend, Tracy Moore, are there to crew and pace her. Whenever Scotty has run an important race, usually Angela and Tracy are there to crew and pace him. In 2021, Scotty (at age 70) recorded his 10th career finish at the impossibly difficult Hardrock 100, which features 33,050 feet of climbing, 33,050 feet of descent, and often has violent thunder and lightning storms that pummel the exposed peaks of the San Juan Mountains of Colorado. Angela was one of his pacers for that race. The same scenario played out when Scotty recorded his 20th Western States finish in 2019. When it came time for Scotty to step down after more than a decade of serving as race director for the San Diego 100, he passed the race director reins to who else? Angela. Scotty's circle grew when he agreed to let Angela run the race she never showed up to run. And Angela has never forgotten it. Their friendship is a reminder that as we age, and if we are lucky and remain open to the possibility, we can continue to make friends throughout our lives and find in their aspirations and goals a renewal of the excitement and energy we once felt when we were younger.

Wise Companions Make Great Mentors

I had no idea that my run at Western States in 2000 and my chance meeting and rescue in the high country by a kind stranger would lead to more than two decades of friendship and mentorship from Scott Mills. It was how Scotty lived his life, and how he welcomed others into his life, which had such a profound effect on me. As we ran together that day, his belief in me became like the pair of hands he had used to lift me after my fall just outside of Red Star Ridge. I could feel their power and their presence even after we parted ways for good not far from the Rucky Chucky river crossing near mile 78. I knew I was on pace for a breakthrough performance. There had been a magical moment a few miles earlier, when we had been running through a part of the course known as "Sandy Bottom," at about mile 75. The waters of the American River come within maybe a stone's throw of the Western States Trail. Because of the high flows of the spring, the trail goes from hard-packed peach-colored dirt to gray sediment. It feels for several hundred yards that you are running on a beach, your movements becoming clumsy like a tourist who clings to a chair and cooler and slips, stumbles, and tries not to faceplant into the sand. Whitewater outfitters often run this portion of the Middle Fork of the American River, and a few miles upstream are the clearly visible Class IV rapids "Chunder" and the Class V+ rapids "Rucky-a-Chucky Falls," which to the uninitiated looks like water raging for its life through a tight sieve of coffin-shaped rocks.

Along Sandy Bottom, however, the river widens, calms, and moves at a meandering pace. If you stop as the sun is starting to go down, you can hear the water easing and petting the shore with a gentle murmur. As I ran along Sandy Bottom in 2000, a whitewater raft and its occupants flowed easily down the river next to me, not more than 75 or 80 yards away. It was early evening by then. Although it was still light, the sun was dropping at the far end of the canyon. The shadows of the trail, stretched uncomfortably by a hot day, were now losing their length, suggesting that it was time to perhaps relax for a minute and to think about the day.

One of the occupants of the whitewater raft called over to me.

"How long have you been out running?"

"Pretty much all day," I yelled back to him.

I smiled and waved to him.

"Us, too," he said. He stood up, his legs uneasy in the slow-moving rubber boat. He raised with a joking solemnity what looked like a can of beer in my honor. "We're going to be done soon."

"Me, too," I said. It was the first time all day long that I had allowed myself to think ahead, to admit that I was nearing the homestretch.

This was a race that I would finish much faster than I had planned, in 21 hours and 51 minutes. I finally had my coveted silver belt buckle. Scotty finished in 22:33.

At the finish line, we had a happy reunion.

"You kept going, and you made it," Scotty said.

He was tired, but Scotty still managed to flash that remarkably white-toothed grin of his, which took me back with its strobe-like brilliance, like the flash of a camera, to that moment near Red Star where I had almost given up.

Then we embraced. I felt the same strong and sure hands that had lifted me up more than 18 hours earlier in the high country. I've never forgotten since then the power of a helping hand, what it means to stop and help another person, to lift them up when they need it most. In any race I've ever run since then, if I see a person fall on the trail, I try to do what Scott Mills did for me. I try to lift that person up. I try to tell them everything is going to be OK. I tell them with the same certainty that Scotty demonstrated to me at the 2000 Western States, that if they can keep going, they are going to make it. And that maybe, just maybe, their life may never be the same again.

CHAPTER 3

No One Else **Like Him**

Most people who knew Roland Martin loved him, although I'm sure most would admit that when they first met him, they weren't quite sure if he even liked them. He did love them, of course. It was just so hard to tell sometimes. Roland was a person of so few words, you could run dozens of miles with him and not hear him utter a single word. He would be there next to you—and this point was extremely important in understanding him—he was always *there* with you, for you, running shirtless. His chest was one of the hairiest things you'd ever seen in your life. He would run in running shorts that were often so tight they appeared to have a time-traveling quality to them, somehow skipping back a few decades and harkening back to the short-shorts era of the 1980s. He gripped in a stout fist a hand-held water bottle held together not with one of those fancy insulated and spacious zippered pockets that can hold numerous gels and car keys aplenty, but rather with withered duct tape. When he'd stop to take a drink, you could see the stringy ends of the duct tape rustling like the chin hair of a goat. Roland was dark-haired and ruggedly handsome, short, and powerfully built like a shirtless fire hydrant, and he was one of the earliest ultra runners my hometown of Reno had ever seen.

It would be tempting to say that Roland's strength was in the fact that he had uncommonly strong legs and a thick upper torso that still reminded those who had known him for a long time of the outstanding football player he'd been while playing collegiately at Sacramento State. He was toughness personified. He rarely, if ever, used pain meds of any kind when he got his dental work done. But in reality, like a lot of things about Roland, you had to look much deeper to see what was actually there. Roland's strength as an ultra runner was his ability to not be intimidated in any way by the long distances he ran. With every hundred-miler he ever entered, he only saw possibilities and an eventual finish. Roland didn't ever look particularly fast and didn't check many of the physical or physiological boxes of what you'd expect of a highly successful and influential ultra runner. That never bothered him. Roland never felt limited. He didn't expect those who he knew, befriended, and mentored (people like me who were lucky enough to be under his wing) to feel any differently either.

"Yes," was always the answer Roland gave when someone asked him about whether they were capable of achieving a goal or running a great distance. His "yes" was never shortened, made loosey-goosey, or contracted with the more informal "yeah." It was always "yes." Roland always lived in the meaningful interpretation one could make when there was plenty of silence in any conversation. And then when pressed further after a long silence, he might add, a bit put out, as if adding words was a frill or an extravagance, "Of course you can." This was the curt chorus we always heard from Roland, whenever we went to him and wondered what we were capable of achieving.

Yes. Of course you can.

I can still hear Roland's voice speaking those words, even today. He was a man of few words, so it is ironic that whenever I have doubts, I can always hear him speaking. His words, and especially those five words, when spoken, meant everything to anyone who ever knew him.

I knew about Roland well before I ever ran an ultra. As a young sportswriter, I'd often cover youth sports during the summertime. It must've been around 1989 or 1990 when I went to a Junior Olympics qualifying meet at Mackay Stadium on the University of Nevada, Reno campus. There were many notable performances that day, but the one that stood out was watching Roland and his daughter Shannon interact before, during, and after Shannon's distance race. Shannon was probably around 12 then. She was one of the better runners for the local youth running club, the Silver State Junior Striders. She was a tall girl who shared the same dark eyebrows of her father, and she ran with such determined focus that her long arms swung back and forth, willing her not to slow. Shannon didn't have a big kick. But she was rare for young age group runners in that her racing was even-paced and not full of the wild impulses of some of her other competitors. She would reach her top speed and then hold that pace and not slow down. That was the way Roland always counseled others to run, too. Watching the two of them, father and daughter, fascinated me. After her race, Shannon could've easily gone off with her teammates. She chose to hang out with her taciturn father, who wasn't the easiest guy in the world to hang out with. Roland was constantly on the move, and that day he moved about the stands and the infield of the track with a quick walk that was both serious and steadfast, a walk that forced Shannon to move after her dad in a light trot. Shannon is 46 years old now, a successful anesthesiologist who graduated with honors from our medical school here in Reno. She has run dozens of ultras, as has her older sister, Jenny. And like so many of us, she felt from an early age a special pull that her father had upon her. Roland made you want to follow him because his footsteps were always treading ground that few had ever experienced before. To be near him, or to have to follow in the wake of that incredibly fast walk of his, watching his strides become so short and so fast they eventually were like a washing machine stuck on spin cycle, was always to feel a vibration of expectation in the air. A sense that there was always something important about to happen whenever you were at the track, on the trails, or simply near Roland.

Roland ran his first Western States in 1985, when he was 36. The experience wasn't ideal. Roland only learned he was in that year's race 10 days before. He was running maybe 30 miles per week at the time. He finished in 28:50, and years later when he talked about the race, he called it a "disaster, though I learned from it." The experience changed running in my hometown forever. What Roland learned was that it might help to have a "hometown" race in Reno that might mimic some of Western States' severe undulations, high altitude in the high country, and more than occasional rockiness. Along with a couple of other local ultra runners, Roland co-founded the Silver State 50-miler, which was held for the first time the following spring in 1986. It became a staple for any runner from northern Nevada or northern California who was entered in Western States or any of that season's major hundred-milers in the region. Silver State was about as "old school" as you could get. There wasn't a lot of fanfare connected to it. Random rocks on the course were spray-painted blue by Roland to signify the 10- and 40-mile marks. Once the agency that had issued the permit to allow the race to be held, the United States Forest Service's Carson Ranger District, learned of this practice, Roland and the race organizers were sternly told to cease and desist the blue spray painting of rocks. Roland, who was an attorney, grudgingly agreed to stop his spray painting.

In addition to co-founding what is today the oldest ultramarathon in Nevada and one of the oldest ultras on the West Coast, held every May since 1986, Roland also was an explorer and a pathfinder. I remember running with him in the 1990s, and how he had an encyclopedic knowledge of the history of every trail, or possible trail, that was in and around the Reno area. Whenever we'd run on the shoulder-shaped Peavine Mountain, which from far away looks brown and dry and without any distinguishing features, Roland's stories of its history would entrance me. I came to know Peavine not as a mountain that I trained on often but as a living, breathing being because of Roland. It became "Mother Peavine" to me because of him. Yes, ultra runners loved running on Peavine because of its steep climbs off its north and west slopes, which were easily accessed, as well as its hard-earned 8,266-foot summit. But there was so much more to it, which Roland would point out during our runs. The towering aspens with the carvings from Basque sheepherders who had run their flocks on the mountain in the 1890s. The spring wildflowers and the wildlife, the long-eared owls, blue grouse, quail, hawks, golden eagles, coyotes, and the mule deer, who seek their winter forage there. I never knew until I heard it from Roland that it was a tiny wild pea, *Vicia americana*, which was one of the reasons why the mountain was called "Peavine" by Reno's white settlers in the first place. And Roland understood we weren't the first people to ever run these Peavine trails. He'd talk of the Paiute people who moved up and down the mountain, which they called "Akiaibi," or "Sunflower Mountain," from the banks of the Truckee River down in the Truckee Meadows and up the shoulders of Mother Peavine, following deer and elk herds. Some of the boulders the first people used as hunting blinds, the rock like the gray humped backs of whales, dating back more than 1,000 years, still stand sentry on the mountain.

"This is a place," Roland once said on one of our runs, "where you don't need to imagine anything. It's all right here for you to see it."

I've often thought about those words and how Roland was very much about the here-and-now. Like a lot of young men from the late 1960s, Roland served in the Army, as a medic in a Green Beret unit in Vietnam. He used even fewer words talking about his experiences there. He earned medals and commendations for acts of bravery. But he never spoke about them. For many different reasons, we all craved the peace and solitude of "Mother Peavine" after a tough day or rough week at work. But Roland, I think, craved his time with "Mother Peavine" more than most of us. It was a place that didn't ask you to dwell in your memories. It was all right there for you to see it.

Yes, Of Course You Can

Roland spent a lot of time running all of the trails in and around Reno, taking in their physical attributes, noting in his lawyer's mind that usually dealt with corporate and tax law the aspects of these runs he wanted to learn more about. He devoted a lot of his energy to old maps and property documents to learn what families had owned what parcels in Reno. Trails or routes came to be known by some of the names of the pioneer families who had come to Reno in the late 19th and early 20th century: the Gaspari Loop and the Ballardini Loop, for example. Such running immersion, where mountains and trails took on their own personalities and had their own histories based on painstaking, time-intensive research, was not surprising to those who knew and loved Roland. He had taken up running in 1979, not long after he'd graduated from law school. His wife, Judy, whom he had married in 1969 while he was still in the Army, discovered early on that she would have to share Roland with running. His ultra running, which he began in 1984 at the Jed Smith 50-miler in Sacramento, meant that Judy would have to be even more patient as Roland spent more time with this silently alluring "second wife." There were times that tried Judy's patience, like the time Roland was due home after he'd gone for a run in Dog Valley on the Nevada-California border. He got his car stuck in the snow in a pretty little valley that is criss-crossed with deep creeks not far from Henness Pass Road, the road that the ill-fated Donner Party followed from the Truckee Meadows into the Sierra in the fall of 1846. Judy grew from not being worried at all, saying, "That's typical Roland, always running late to an event after going for a run," to becoming concerned and calling friends to mount an impromptu Dog Valley search party for her husband. They eventually found Roland running down Dog Valley Road back into Reno, clad only in a T-shirt, shorts, and running shoes. Stories like that one became part of the mythology that surrounded Roland. He always showed up, he always got the day's run in, no matter if he came perilously close to disappearing into the Sierra the same way the Donner Party did. There was an appealing kind of Sisyphean logic to Roland's running that always resonated with those of us who ran with him. If you missed a day, or if you didn't do what was expected of you, there was always a chance that the rock you were trying to push up the mountain of your training might slip or roll backwards a few inches. At the very least, Roland's quiet example of always being there illustrated to us that we had to show up. Very few times did Roland ever leave showing up to chance. There was one race where he forgot to bring his running shoes. He had driven to the race wearing sandals. Why turn around and drive home when you could run the race in your sandals? Which Roland, of course, did.

In 2000, I asked Roland to pace me at Western States. I hemmed and hawed about my chances as I made the ask of him: "If I can just get to Foresthill where you can pick me up and pace me, I'm hoping to make a run at breaking 24 hours. What do you think?" It was a fortuitous choice. I got more than a pacer. I got a much-needed confidence boost from a seasoned runner whose time in the sport went almost back to its infancy. Roland could eye other runners the way a wily horse trainer could inspect all racehorses and with a blink of an eye spot any competitive imperfections. Roland's response: "Yes." And then I waited. He added again, "Yes," as if it should be more than enough to allay any doubts I might have. It was later, when he was there for me, that I felt the other words: Of course you can. Of course you can break 24 hours. It's not just a matter of breaking of 24 hours, but by how much you're going to do it. Roland inferred all of this simply and unequivocally. So not only had I met Scotty Mills, who had helped me to my feet in the high country, I had perhaps the most knowledgeable pacer in the entire race running with me for the final 38 miles. Roland and Scotty were contemporaries. They had run in the same races since the early 1980s, and it was obvious they held each other in high esteem. When Scotty and I parted ways near the river crossing at mile 78, Roland, running shirtless and in his tight-tight shorts, complimented me on my good fortune in meeting Scotty.

"You made a good trail friend today," Roland said as we began the long hike up from the American River to the 80-mile mark at Green Gate. "Scotty's a smart ultra runner. You need to stay friends with the smart ultra runners. Not the dumb ones." We got a good laugh out of that one. And a little later, I told Roland that his words, however brief, had always carried immense meaning to me. When he had said, "Yes," months earlier, acknowledging with one simple world how expansive he thought my capabilities as a runner were, a lot had changed for me.

"It meant a lot to me that you said you thought I could do it," I said.

Roland, running a few strides ahead of me, turned and looked over his shoulder at me, flashing one of his shy smiles at me.

"It meant a lot to me that you asked," he said softly.

As we made it past 80 miles, then 85 miles, Roland's method of pacing was to keep pushing me. I would see his hairy, sweat-stained back move into the milky light of my flashlight. He would linger for a moment, then look over his shoulder at me, his dark eyes measuring me. Then he would run ahead of me. First a few yards. Then 25, then 50 yards ahead. He expected me to keep up with him, even as I did the calculations and realized that barring unforeseen disaster, I was going to break 24 hours. Each time I would grunt and groan and mildly curse Roland's name under my breath and force myself to catch back up to him as the shock fatigue of running that great of distance pounded like a cudgel through my entire body. There was a moment where Roland was so far ahead of me that all I saw was his impatient flashlight, nervously swatting at the air, beckoning me to fight the urge to slow, reminding me that you need to go hard in a race like Western States or else risk having it come back to bite you later on. Roland knew all about my 96-second disappointment from three years before, and in the darkness, just far enough out of my sight to be either my guardian pacer or an apparition of my past failure, he knew that I needed to run unguarded and unburdened by what happened in 1997. I kept chasing his flashlight and, in so doing, cast away my fears.

Roland was right. Yes. Of course I could. And when we finished, the first thing Roland did after he congratulated me was to seek out a lawn chair. He plopped right down into it, bare-chested and sweaty, his flashlight dropping into his lap like a useless little toy as those strong hands of his suddenly looked extremely vulnerable and tired. He smiled at me. He appeared to be every one of his 51 years. He had given pacing me his all. He looked utterly spent. I hadn't realized until that moment how much of an emotional investment Roland always made, for all of us.

History Made

A few months later, Roland and his friends, Joe Braninburg and Robert Sobsey, made history. They were the first runners to ever complete successfully what was then the 152-mile Tahoe Rim Trail (today it measures 171 miles), finishing in 66 hours. The three friends started under a full moon at around 4 a.m. on September 13 at the Mount Rose Trailhead, which is about a 25-minute drive from Reno. Over the next two and a half days, they ran together and experienced what often happens when there are three people involved with such an effort. There were times when Roland or Robert would drag behind Joe, who was the faster ultra runner of the three. Robert, a highly organized person who for years had served in Washoe County as a health inspector, remembered his blistered feet had become so painful toward the end, he began to fantasize about dropping off the trail, located high on the ridgetops above Lake Tahoe, and sprinting down to the specks of lights of the homes nestled on Lake Tahoe's shores that were miles below the trail. It felt more worth it, Robert said, given his accumulated fatigue and how many miles of the narrow trail that were still left, to abandon their quest for the off-chance that someone in the homes below would be awake, and that after a knock at their front door at 2 a.m. they would welcome a stinky, unshaved stranger with the deranged eyes of someone who had been in the wild a little too long. "It was," Robert told me later, "the worst and best kind of ultra challenge. You didn't want to go on. You started to really wonder why you were up there tripping along the trail. But you didn't want to give up on it, either."

Roland, who was always chronically underdressed for the coldest conditions, became borderline hypothermic at one point near Armstrong Pass above Lake Tahoe's south shore. The wind had picked up, night was falling, and the high-altitude temperatures were rapidly dropping. In only shorts and T-shirt and shivering uncontrollably, Roland scrambled right into a tent and into a waiting sleeping bag set up by a couple of surprised campers. The next morning, Roland popped out of the sleeping bag, refreshed and ready to run as if nothing had happened. "It was one of those mornings," he told me later, "like in the old days where you wake up and from the first step on, you run the way you always want to run." Joe remembered that as Roland took the lead from them that day, "Roland looked like he was never going to slow down . . . or look back to check on us, for that matter. He had the eye of the tiger that day. We had to sprint like hell to keep up with him."

They finished together at the Mount Rose Trailhead, at 10:20 p.m. on September 15, 2000.

In July 2013, Roland's oldest daughter, Jenny, set the women's supported fastest-known time on the TRT with a 53-hour effort. She ran with a photo of a bearded and young Roland, sitting in a chair after he had finished the 1988 Western States, pinned to the back of her gray hydration vest. Jenny and her father were a lot alike. Jenny could be stubborn like her father, and her willingness to push herself was far beyond the norm of most ultra runners. She was married to a fellow physical therapist, Steve, and had two spirited sons. She was also like her father in that she often followed her own path. Jenny has always been an accomplished runner, an elite-level competitor who for over two decades recorded times at the 50- and 100-mile distances that remain some of the fastest ever run. Yet she has never chased after recognition or sponsorships. She has eschewed social media posts and putting herself "out there," opting instead for the purity of running her races freely. "Jenny has always been so much like her father in so many ways," Judy said. "She has never been afraid to challenge herself. And she is stubborn. So stubborn. Just like her father." There has also always been a surprising tenderness to her. One year at Western States, she failed to finish. She didn't quite know how her father, who had always pushed himself to the brink in order to get to every finish line, would react. Roland didn't judge. He listened as Jenny talked about her race. Like all of Roland's best moments, what wasn't said was what mattered. Jenny realized that it was the fact that her father was there with her, listening, that had always mattered.

So when Jenny set her TRT record in 2013 with Roland's photo pinned to the back of her vest, it was the fact that he was there again with her that mattered. She said after she finished that it was her intent to have her dad experience the TRT with her, "only a little faster."

Sometimes the Toughest Races Are Run Off the Trail

We all knew that Roland was facing a major health battle by the time Jenny set her TRT record in 2013. He had been diagnosed with a form of brain cancer by then, one that severely impacted his balance and necessitated several procedures and treatment. Judy was always there by his side, helping lead him on short walks and outings, keeping him involved with the many activities of his family. In addition to Jenny's children, there were also son Shawn's as well. Despite the physical limitations he was facing, Roland whole-heartedly stayed as involved in the lives of his grandchildren as he had when Jenny, Shannon, and Shawn were growing up. He had been his children's first coach, whether it was in running or softball or basketball, and though he had always walked briskly and was hard to keep up with throughout the course of their many activities, the fact of the matter was they all three knew that Roland was the type of father who would never wish to leave any of his children behind. In fact, if anything, he had always been like that light I had chased after in June 2000 at Western States, that light that was just ahead on the trail, that light that calls to us to join it because it earnestly believes that we belong with it.

He came to the finish line of the race I had inherited as race director, the race he had co-founded back in 1986, Silver State, with his head nearly completely shaved due to the treatments he'd been receiving, another year with what looked like a brace wrapped around his waist with a short line held by Judy that helped keep him upright, and watched all of the runners as they finished their journeys on Peavine, the mountain he loved, on the course he had created. When he saw my daughters, Annie and Katie, who had both spent a long day on the mountain trouble-shooting, running miles and miles of shortcuts to and from the course to ensure that all of our race's directional ribbons hadn't been removed, their faces covered in dust and the flour they had used to mark key turns, Roland smiled with a quiet contentment like a man who realized his influence had been successfully passed on to the next generation. Annie and Katie had both been coached by Roland when they were in high school. And they, too, were people who by being around Roland had learned that communities are only built through the actions of those who are willing to give, whose natural tendency for esprit de corps is amplified by the honest acts done in the service of others. And by those who had spent days like Annie and Katie had just experienced on the flanks of a cold mountain, spraying flour arrows on the ground, and checking ribbons flapping stiffly in a hard wind, just because you didn't want any runners to get lost. They were following in Roland's footsteps, quietly and reliably, as we all had tried to do over the years.

Of course, there was no one else like him. There was only one Roland. There was only one person who could say so little yet influence so many.

Roland kept going until he passed away, at his home under the love and care of his family, at age 69, on April 27, 2018.

It was during the pandemic, on July 4, 2020, that Katie and I took a long run up to Hunter Lake, which isn't so much a lake as it is a seasonal wetland lined by willows that at its wettest might be about the size of a football field. It is slightly above 8,000 feet elevation, and it isn't reached easily, coming after a more than 3,000-foot climb of seven miles of jeep road that is so rocky, you have to pause to figure out where the road is actually going. There are amazing aspens and boulders the size of UPS vans that line rutted Hunter Lake Road. For years, Hunter Lake, named after John Hunter, who operated a toll to cross it, had been the beginning of the long descent to the finish of Silver State. Katie and I continued on past Hunter Lake, the road narrowing, the sage, tobacco brush, and currant giving way to towering lodgepole pine trees and a stream that opened into another meadow. Not far from there, half-buried but still visible, was a blue rock that used to be the 40-mile mark of Silver State. It was one of Roland's rocks. A reminder that one of the most important responsibilities a person can ever have, when someone comes to you and asks if a dream is attainable, is to answer affirmatively. To always do what Roland had done, to respond with "Yes," and then, after the appropriate time had passed to mull the transformative power of that one word to influence the direction of a life, to then add, "Of course you can."

CHAPTER 4

The Secret Ingredient of Success: **The Women of Western States**

When the history of the Western States Endurance Run is shared, it is usually told through a male-centric lens. Wendell Robie, born of pioneer stock, was the visionary godfather who not only wished to bring an old immigrant gold country trail back to life, but wanted it, in the same way that a thousand years ago all roads led to Rome, to lead right into his hometown of Auburn, California. Gordy Ainsleigh was the quirky woodcutter who had enough audacious belief in his athletic abilities to think that it was possible to cover on foot the entire 100-mile distance from Olympic Valley, California to Auburn, California in less than 24 hours. And then from there, almost like magic, one of the world's most well-known and prestigious endurance events was born.

Subscribing to this version of history comes at a real cost. It conveniently leaves out the integral role that women have played in making Western States what it is today. It has been the women of Western States who were the ones who gave the race its staying power. Whenever anyone who has ever run the race talks about the experience, they speak of it in reverential, transformational terms. "It changed my life," they say. "I was a different person, a better person, because I ran the race," they say. "It reminded me of what was important, essential, to a life that has some meaning," they say. And all of this has little to do with who the first-place finisher of a particular year was. It has everything to do, however, with how an idea to run 100 miles through the mountains of the Sierra became real. And how the race in its infancy was incredibly lucky to have a couple of women give it a soul, a heart, a sense of attainable mystery that wraps every Western States runner in a blanket that they never, even after they finish and the years pass, ever fully shed. Whenever a runner had any doubts about finishing, there had to be someone who could assure them. Whenever someone called on the telephone from across the country inquiring about this strange, crazy race they had heard about, there had to be a voice on the other end who enthusiastically sang the new endeavor's praises. For anyone who dared to dream about running 100 miles, there had to be a human connection made first, one that boiled the distance down to its barest necessity—that Western States wasn't just a 100-mile race. It was a human race.

Joining Forces

They were called "Mo-Shan," which was a combination of their first names and a very apt description of what they created whenever they were together. Mo Livermore and Shannon Weil could not be more different in personal background, in personality, in the particular set of skills that each woman possesses. When their involvement with Western States began in the late 1970s, what was a fledgling idea became a reality.

Marion "Mo" Livermore's connection to California went back generations. Her family's history was one that felt like it belonged on the pages of Joan Didion, whose writing has always made the Golden State feel like a primary character with particular virtues and a sense that even with the constant change that is California, it is always possible to get a feeling for the way things used to be. Mo's father, William H. Orrick, Jr., was a United States District Judge and a former Assistant U.S. Attorney General under President John F. Kennedy. Her grandfather, Dr. Howard Naffziger, was a world-renowned neurosurgeon who, following World War I, founded the Department of Neurosurgery at the University of California Medical School. She came from families who believed in the power of "can do" that could trace their time in California back practically to the Gold Rush. Mo was herself a graduate of the University of California, acutely aware of the history of her state. As a young woman she sought out a slightly different and independent path from those in her family who had come before. She was a horse lover and matriculated to some of the best horse country in the entire state in and around the trail-clutching golden hills of Auburn, California. She rode the Tevis Cup for the first time in 1972.

Shannon Yewell Weil had always been a bit of a bohemian. She grew up in Altadena, California in a home where artistry and the arts were always welcomed. Her mother, Nancy Dau Yewell, impressed upon Shannon from an early age the value of volunteering. "Never miss an opportunity," Nancy would cheerily tell her daughter. Nancy was in many ways the ultimate volunteer. When she died in 1983, Nancy had spent more than two decades as an indispensable volunteer at the Pasadena Art Museum, chair of the Docent Council, member of the Pasadena Art Alliance, and founder and chair of the grassroots arts organization Fellows of Contemporary Art. She was constantly championing the efforts of contemporary West Coast artists. Shannon was a talented and creative person herself who could write, sketch, and paint. From her mother's warm welcoming of various artists of all of the contemporary genres, Shannon learned that artistry and self-expression were two of the most important ways a person could ever live and have a positive impact on those around them. She would find this especially valuable as her life progressed. When she was 19, Shannon, who had always loved horses, learned from the famed rider Linda Tellington-Jones, who in a gentle, reassuring, collaborative and positive way, was just as effective influencing human beings as she was horses. By 1976, Shannon, who first rode the Tevis Cup in 1969, was a crew member for an epic adventure, the Great American Horse Race and Pony Express Ride, which over the space of about three months in the summer of the nation's bicentennial in 1976 took the participating riders the 3,500 miles between New York and California.

The paths of the two young women crossed in the world of trail riding. But it was the prospect of helping runners that brought the two of them together. For Shannon, it was the experience of riding in the Western States Trail Ride in 1977 that would change everything for her. It was the same year that the first official Western States Endurance Run was held with 14 runners who started along with the horses. "The memory brings back chills to me," Shannon said. She was leaving the 55-mile mark at Michigan Bluff. It so happened that the runner leading the run that day, 22-year-old Andy Gonzales, was also leaving Michigan Bluff at the same time. Andy Gonzales was a handsome, dark-haired young man who ran so effortlessly, it was impossible to tell if he had just run 55 miles or five miles. He carried no water bottles and had no food with him. Following behind Andy on her horse, Shannon began to think of the lessons she had learned at the nurturing school where she had learned about horses and life from Linda Tellington-Jones.

"Andy was just sort of gutting it out," Shannon said. "He was this dark-haired stranger, and we were leap-frogging back and forth. Here was this tiny seedling of an event, this event where runners were daring themselves to run 100 miles, and it became this very poignant moment in my life as I watched Andy running. I had been taught by the Tellingtons to always think big. And wrapping that thought into my background in art, self-expression, and the wonder of creating something wonderful, I really saw what the vision for the race could be. That's exactly what I began to think as I rode along with Andy. It just completely confirmed to me that this run is going to be a big hit and that I was going to make sure that it was."

Mo was on hand that day as well. She had been recruited by Wendell Robie, who was in his early 80s by then, to help on the run side of the event that year, to time and to generally watch out for the runners. Mo's sense of propriety, of doing things right, safely, and by the book, had always been a defining feature. Already the wheels were turning in her mind about what she was witnessing. In the years that were to come, as Mo took on the responsibilities of being the race director along with Shannon throughout the late 1970s and into the early 1980s, she would seek out people who could be trusted to watch out for the welfare of the runners who were embarking on a journey marked by unknowns and uncertainties. These were the people who would become the core of the Western States volunteer structure and would set an incredibly high standard in their devotion to the event. Placer County Sheriff Department Captain Marvin Jacinto, whose everyday life in law enforcement centered on serving as the department's Patrol Commander and coordinator of the County Search and Rescue Team, became an indispensable presence at Western States. Thanks to Jacinto's belief in the race and his strong sense of duty, in the early years of the race, search and rescue units were stationed throughout many of the most remote sections of the course. During that day in August 1977 when she shadowed the progress of the 14 runners who were entered, Mo was paired with a kind, grey-haired emergency room doctor from Roseville, California, Dr. Robert Lind, who carried not much more than a thermometer, a blood pressure kit, and a constant, encouraging smile with him as he monitored the runners' vital signs and weight at a handful of medical checkpoints. In Dr. Lind, the runners had an uncommonly inquisitive person looking out for them. In the years to come, Dr. Lind would welcome medical researchers from throughout the world to come to Western States to observe and study the world's longest endurance performance laboratory.

The race's winner, Andy Gonzales, was not a surprise champion. His lithe running form would never leave him that day. The other two finishers that day, unlike Gonzales, did not have the advantage of ample youth on their side. They would need an additional four and a half hours beyond the race's 24-hour cutoff time to finish. They were told on at least a couple of occasions that they would have to be responsible for their own food, water, and aid. And yet, Dr. Ralph Paffenbarger, 54, and Peter Mattei, 53, chose not to stop. Mo was struck that day by how the two friends, both men in their 50s, seemed more like graying Greatest Generation fathers than competitive athletes.

"Ralph would trot lightly in, big smile on his face, raving about the scenery and what a great day it was to be running the Western States Trail," Mo said. "I think they both knew what an amazing day they were having."

Their journey to Auburn was completed in 28:36. Remarkably, with only a few hours to rest following their finish that morning, both Paffenbarger and Mattei were able to attend the awards ceremony for the Tevis Cup horse ride. Wendell Robie stopped the awards ceremony and began cheering Paffenbarger and Mattei's accomplishment. It really wasn't very surprising that Robie would recognize two pioneering individuals when he saw them. Robie, too, had been an "older" person of 60 when he had ridden across the Sierra for the first time in 1955. "Wendell profusely raved about the triumph of these two gentlemen to the point that many riders felt their own admirable accomplishments were overshadowed by Ralph and Peter's feat," Shannon said. "It was a remarkable sight indeed."

The first true seeds of what Western States would become were planted that afternoon in 1977. In watching two men who were the same age as her parents finish Western States in under 30 hours, 25-year-old Mo had also seen how having support along the way could bring out extraordinary performances from seemingly ordinary people.

"You can see how those first runners directly impacted the development of the Western States Endurance Run," Mo said. "Peter and Ralph showed, more than any previous finisher, that it really could be done. Ralph and Peter's contributions were more, then, than just creating the prototype of the 30-hour finisher; it was much more about creating the whole race as we know it today. Andy Gonzales showed us that you could be extraordinary and young and complete the distance. Peter and Ralph showed us you could be extraordinary and not so young and also complete the distance."

Shannon went to work for Wendell Robie at the Heart Federal Savings & Loan right after the ride. "I wanted to get as close to the flame as I possibly could," she said. Mo continued on with her charge from Wendell Robie to continue to make a more formal run possible at Western States. In the two young women, as well as Shannon's husband, Phil Gardner, Mo's husband, Curt Sproul, (they came to be known as "The Gang of Four"), and his personal secretary, Drucilla "Dru" Barner, Robie found kindred spirits who shared his love for the

Western States Trail. Robie's Heart Federal became the place where 100-mile trail running dreams were hatched and realized, an epicenter of 100-mile trail running in the United States before he or anyone actually realized it was becoming such a focal point. "It was very much a 'second star on the right, straight on 'til morning,' kind of experience," Mo said. "Wendell always wanted our very best: our very best ideas, our very best ways to make the run something that would last."

Shannon's duties at Heart Federal included being the person who answered the phone when people called from across the country inquiring about this new 100-mile running race, Western States. Shannon took the job seriously. She wanted what would be a simple informational phone call to pack all the meaning and encouragement that it possibly could. "Somebody had to answer the calls," she said. "I was just so excited about what Wendell was handing us. It was an opportunity of a lifetime. I wanted to convey on the phone the magnificence of the trail. I wanted them to feel like they should drop everything and come run the Western States Trail with us. It all just kind of spiraled upward and took off on us in that regard. We loved what Wendell was handing to us, and we reflected it to everyone who came to run the trail.

"We became the Western States Family."

The First Lady of Western States

If there was a person both Mo and Shannon looked to for inspiration, it was Drucilla "Dru" Barner. "Dru," as she was known to those close to her, was an unforgettable presence. She was a small woman with a gracious manner. In the late 1950s, following her divorce from her philandering husband, she moved from the Carson Valley in Nevada. Then she answered an ad to become Wendell Robie's personal secretary at the Heart Federal Savings and Loan Bank in Auburn. Over the decades to come, she did much more than type Robie's correspondence or schedule his day. She became Robie's partner in many of the events that he would play a role in creating, from the Tevis Cup to the Western States Endurance Run. Wrote Robie biographer Bill Wilson of Dru's role in his life, "She had been with him for 21 years, and he considered her almost indispensable. Dru, he felt, had the uncanny ability to make the right decisions when he slipped into tedium and needed a trusted person to take the lead."

Originally from Sausalito, California, Dru was known as one of the finest horse riders, male or female, of her generation. "Understated," Mo recalled. "Dru was outwardly refined, yet very adventurous in her soul." In 1961, Dru became the first woman to ever win the Western States 100-Mile Trail Ride (Tevis Cup). She would complete Tevis 10 times between 1958 and 1974.

It was actually Dru who had encouraged Ainsleigh to take his historic 100-mile run, along with the horses of the Tevis Cup, in 1974. A year earlier, on a training ride during the summer of 1973, Ainsleigh's horse had gone lame. Dejectedly heading up Robie Drive near Dru's home, Ainsleigh saw her tending flowers in her front yard. Dru called out to Gordy and asked what had happened. When told about his lame horse, Dru noted dryly that Gordy, for an equestrian, was starting to spend more time with his feet on the ground than in stirrups. "When are you going to leave your horse behind and do the whole thing on foot?" Dru called to her young friend. "Next year is going to be the 20th anniversary of the ride, and I think that would be a wonderful time for you to just leave your horse in the pasture and run the whole thing." Hearing those words "was kind of like getting an invitation from God," Gordy said.

And it was Dru who was constantly championing Mo and Shannon's abilities. She knew quality when she saw it. She also knew that both young women played off each other's strengths and weaknesses and made for a terrific team. Mo was meticulous, a planner, always aware of runner safety and of the integral role that a network of devoted volunteers would play in the success of the run. "I was always on the lookout for volunteers, for people who had a strong sense that giving back was one of the most important things you can ever do in life," Mo said. She also believed wholeheartedly in what Western States had the potential to do for any person, whether they ran it or volunteered at it. "This is a race that changes a person's life," she said. "I've always believed in the gift of the Western States Trail, that the people who are involved in the race are always touched by it. They grow physically, emotionally, and spiritually because of this great gift we've all been given."

If Western States had been an ad agency, Shannon would've served as creative director. She was constantly imagining what the Western States story needed to be and how it needed to be told in order to capture the imagination of any curious runner from throughout the country who wondered what the event was and what it might take to complete it. In the years to come, Shannon would play an indispensable role in the race's branding, from the design of the regal and beautiful cougar that—thanks to the craftsmanship of first Howard Stegman and now his son, James Stegman—has adorned the finisher's belt buckles for going on five decades now, to the cougar trophy presented each year to the race's winners created originally by the famed Napa, California sculptor Franco Vianello. You could almost hear her mother's guiding words of never missing an opportunity in all the ways Shannon was able to create a rich and vibrant color palette of expectation for Western States. "It was all about sharing and bringing people to the Western States Trail," Shannon said. "And the world rushed in."

The fact that Dru Barner, in particular, supported their efforts meant the world to the two young women.

"Dru gave us her blessing," Shannon said. "She trusted us. With one wave of her hand, she put wind beneath our wings."

Girls to the Front

The first Western States Endurance Run, separate from the ride, was held in 1978. There were more than 60 entrants from states as far away as Texas and Florida, ranging in age and ability from 70-year-old Walt Stack of San Francisco to 18-year-old twins Karin and Peggy Stok of Redwood City, California, to Pat Smythe of Kentfield, California, who would go on to become the only woman that day to finish under the race's official time limit of 30 hours in 29:34. A template of care and attention to the well-being and safety of all the runners had clearly been established by Mo and Shannon. Just one example occurred late in the race, around 3 a.m., when 30-year-old Steve Mason of Sparks, Nevada, wandered off course with only about seven miles remaining. The intricate network of volunteers who were willing to be there for all of the runners throughout the entirety of the event swung into action. Steve was found a few hours later by safety team members John Kessler, Jay Brands, Rod Willard, and a nurse by the name of Carol Van Ness, who for years would help build an impressive group of nurses who would come from neighboring communities each year to lend their expertise and care in the days before, during, and after the event. After Steve was examined by Dr. Lind and another doctor recruited to help, Dr. Gary Towle, who to this day remains a member of the Western States board of trustees, he was allowed to continue, eventually finding the finish in 29:39. Steve's wife Jane later wrote in a letter to the editor in the *Auburn Journal* on July 14, 1978: "Steve and I both learned so much about the mountains and the valleys of California, but the thing we will always remember is the kindness and generosity of the people of the Auburn area."

Mo-Shan had created a caring and thoughtful ethos to a race that would grow rapidly during their time as co-race directors from the late 1970s and into the early 1980s. By 1979, there were 143 entrants, and in 1980, it grew to 251 entrants. The Western States Trail provided the formidable challenge of running 100 miles through the beautiful but incredibly taxing undulations of the Sierra. But it was the people who provided the race with its heart. The medical team of Drs. Lind and Towle and Dr. Gil Lang and Carol Van Ness and her cadre of caring registered nurses grew to more than 125 people by the early 1980s. The search and rescue efforts were led by the skilled Captain Marvin Jacinto, and coordination of a passel of well-trained ham radio operators was headed by Jerry Holm with Betty Veal serving as Race Day Secretary. The aid stations were captained by people who were all about doing all they could to ensure that the runners' dreams of running 100 miles could come true. These were people like Shannon's parents, the irrepressible Nancy and equally enthusiastic George Yewell, who were in charge of the Michigan Bluff aid station just past the halfway mark.

Life would eventually take Shannon and Mo on different paths. Mo would run the race in 1981 and 1983, her time in 1983 good for a sub-24-hour "silver buckle," and remains to this day a member of the Western States board of trustees. Shannon would move for a time to American Samoa in the mid-1980s before returning to the Auburn area. She would rejoin the Western States Board and become a driving force in the creation of Auburn's re-branding and positioning as "The Endurance Capital of the World" in the early 2000s. I've known both Mo and Shannon for more than 20 years now. You cannot have a conversation with either one of them without feeling that you've touched history and that you are in the midst of two trailblazing women who didn't necessarily see themselves as trailblazers at all. What they did as they served as co-race directors of Western States during a time in running history where there were very few female race directors was distill the best of their natures and instill it into a 100-mile race. Shannon has always been fond of telling the story of how she would always watch the nurses, the women like Carol Van Ness, who would take blood pressures and do a quick medical inventory of all Western States' entrants the day before the race was held in Olympic Valley. If you've never been to the Olympic Valley, the site of the 1960 Winter Olympics, it's an awesome place. There is a headwall of peach-colored rock that runs straight up from the green and beautiful valley floor, looming like an unnerving and unscalable rock barrier, marking the foot of civilization and what is comfortable and known to what is unknown and almost unimaginable: the 100 miles of trail that lead runners from Olympic Valley to Auburn. For any potential runners, staring up at the headwall can make blood pressures soar and can make any athletic intentions crash-land into reality. And that was what fascinated Shannon so much. She would see the women, the Carol Van Nesses, comfort the nervous runners. She would see them touch their arms lightly. She would see them smile reassuringly. She would see them impart advice about taking care of yourself, of eating and drinking and the value of a little bit of salt intake throughout the run. She would see them tell the runners that they could do it. That they were worthy of going the distance, and what's more, that they *would* go the distance.

And in my own mind's eye, I see this, and I also see Mo and Shannon as young women, sitting on a quiet late afternoon in the Heart Federal building, nestled off Lincoln Way on a hopeful upslope above downtown Auburn, with Wendell Robie and Dru Barner. Wendell loved vanilla ice cream, and it was often a Heart Federal custom for him to share bowls of vanilla ice cream in the bank with the people he cared about. I can see the four of them, two visionary older people with two excited and equally visionary young women, sitting together and eating vanilla ice cream, Wendell and Dru listening patiently, nodding their encouragement, as Mo and Shannon put forth their many ideas on how they hoped to make Western States special. They have always believed that there is a light that resides in all of us—a light that when kindled, always asks us to do more. All that light ever needs, these two wonderful women of Western States have always thought, is to experience 100 miles on the Western States Trail so that it can be shared with all of us.

PART **TWO**

Choosing Your **Companions**

CHAPTER 5

Running **Free**

Whether it was the case or not, the way Emily Richards appeared in our lives felt almost like we had been blessed by the discovery of a rare type of beautiful butterfly. When we held our local ultra, the Silver State 50-Miler in mid-May 2015, it had started raining the day before and did not let up until a few hours before the 6 a.m. start. The race day itself was marked by more than a little mud and some wind, which required many of our runners to bundle up in layers and to watch every step they took. We had one of the best female ultra runners in the world, Kaci Lickteig of Omaha, Nebraska entered. Kaci would go on to become the 2016 women's champion at Western States. Over the years, Kaci has always been a fan of our race and has run Silver State a few times. She always considered our course with its long climbs, even longer descents, and altitude that reaches close to 8,000 feet to be the perfect preparation for Western States. But on this particular mid-May day in 2015, Kaci was joined at the front of the women's race by a young woman dressed almost completely in black: black tights, black long-sleeve shirt, topped off by a white hat with a big bill that seemed to make her appear even younger than her 35 years.

Fast runners immediately take notice of other fast runners, which was what Kaci did. They were running on mud, and the new runner ran effortlessly over it. Kaci herself is very light on her feet and runs the way an artist would, using her feet to flick across any type of terrain the way a brush flicks on a canvass, bringing it color. The new runner seemed to be in service of something important and ran with a dexterous joy. Her arms would pump out at her sides like the wings of a bird preparing to take flight whenever the mud became too much. She never lost her balance, never hinted at being distressed by the quick pace the two were maintaining. It was as if the trail was a muddy keyboard, and the new runner's feet were like a pair of finely honed fingers belonging to a classical pianist. The trail was like music to the new runner, and she read it with uncommon grace and confidence.

It can take runners hours or seconds to start a conversation on the trail, and for the two runners, as they came upon each other about half-way through the 50-mile race, it was the latter.

"We started talking, and she was just so nice," Kaci remembered. "She said she knew who I was [Kaci had finished sixth at Western States the year before, in 2014, in her Western States debut.] and that she was grateful to be sharing the trail with me. I remember asking Emily what her name was and what races she had done.

"Emily was so humble, saying she had done some ultra marathons. She never boasted, never let on about anything she'd done. She was just so cheerful and fun to run with and was just so graceful as we ran effortlessly down the trail.

"You run across bright lines in our world, and Emily was definitely one of them."

Emily Richards would eventually—and very politely—wish Kaci luck and thank her for the time spent together. She would then proceed to run away from one of the world's top ultra runners that day. At the River Bend aid station, near the 32-mile mark, Emily's father, Tom, sporting a green vest with Levi's and carrying a cowbell, greeted his daughter with a spirited cowbell clang and opened his arms to her for a quick hug.

"It was a most awesome and unexpected surprise," Emily said later of Tom's appearance. "His image slowly coming into view as I was dropping into River Bend. That's Dad! These are the best days, when I feel elated by the inspiration and kindness of fellow runners, volunteers, and family."

Emily would go on to win the women's race, finish second overall, and finish in a time that was only a few minutes slower than when the legendary 14-time Western States women's champion Ann Trason had run in Reno more than two decades before. When she finished, Emily made a point to thank me, the race director, for such a great event and for all of the great volunteers who had staffed the day's aid stations.

"It was so much fun," she said, and not long after, she was joined by her husband, Colin, and her father. Emily lingered by the finish line until Kaci finished, and the two young women embraced and congratulated each other on good races.

"You smoked it!" Kaci told Emily, with a huge smile.

I still had no idea who Emily Richards was.

Winning at What Cost?

Emily Richards' story is one of understanding that what you love can sometimes come at a great cost. If you have a talent for something like running, and you love running with all of your heart, it can hurt when there are detours, illness, or injury. Running can seem less like something that is cherished and more a source of torment and distress. Part of this can be because you experience success in running. You feel that you've solved the riddle without truly understanding what the answer is. You run with athletic earnestness, with all of your might, and feel it is homage enough when you win or post a fast time. But then you learn that with the passage of time, there can be disruptions and frustrations. It can become like running into the same endless wall, each collision taking something away that you feel you might not ever get back. What happened with Emily's running at an early age wasn't weakness or some kind of personal shortcoming. She developed a health condition that many young people can develop, one that nearly killed her. Years later she could see all of the signs were there: the increasing sense of isolation, of hopelessness, of limiting food intake because of the insecurities involved with wondering how others thought about her. It's hard to see through all of that when you are 14 years old. It can sometimes take years before you realize that you have always been a good and virtuous person, and that you've always possessed many talents that can bring order and clarity and purpose to the lives of other people. And it can take years to make peace with your running after illness and injury, to understand that there is nothing given about an activity that can often ask a lot of you. The understanding of all of this would come, slowly and painfully, over the course of many years for Emily. Part of her healing, which also required hospitalization, counseling, and a reestablishment of two-way trust in her familial relationships, came when she happened to meet a man who, like her, had felt some personal pain himself in his own life.

There was an honest vulnerability that Colin Chisholm saw in Emily Richards, almost from the first time he met her. In 2012, Emily was studying to apply to nursing school in Reno. She was living in a studio apartment above a garage in Truckee, California, owned by Colin's brother, Brad. Colin was in his early 40s then. He'd been living in Missoula, Montana, working as a hospice social worker and psychotherapist. He had grown up in Lake Tahoe, in Olympic Valley, the site of the 1960 Winter Olympic Games, a place that to this day reflects the tension that was created by that momentous moment. Alexander Cushing, the founder of the ski corporation known today as Palisades Tahoe, had through sheer force of a magnetic and obstinate personality brought the Winter Games to a tiny, bucolic valley nestled halfway between the magnificent blue waters of Lake Tahoe and the nearby railroad town of Truckee. There was no easy way in and out of Olympic Valley. There were actually, other than a great ski run that swooped down from great granite peaks that thousands of travelers had crossed during the Gold Rush on what was then called the Auburn-Placer Emigrant Road, no Olympic facilities that had been built at the site when Olympic Valley was awarded the Olympic Games in 1956. It didn't matter. If they built it, Alex Cushing always believed, the world would come. With the help of the State of California, the United States Olympic Committee, and an amalgam of star power that included Walt Disney's participation in creating Opening Ceremonies that included the release of more than 2,000 doves, Olympic Valley became the picture-perfect winter postcard that Cushing had envisioned for the world to see.

Colin had grown up in the same valley. He and his family were part of a group of residents who also saw the postcard that Cushing had shared with the world (a postcard that seemed so American because venerable CBS News anchor Walter Cronkite had been on sight during the Opening Ceremonies) and the growth that followed, and felt instead that the valley had been violated, its beauty in danger of being lost. Colin had members of his family who could trace their lineage to the Yup'ik people of Alaska and wrote movingly about it in his 2000 book, *Through Yup-ik Eyes: An Adopted Son Explores the Landscape of Family*, and these experiences helped shape who he was to become. His mother, in particular, had taken great pains to teach her son about Olympic Valley's wonders. She would often take him on long hikes up Shirley Canyon, into a wilderness of rocky granite chutes and waterfalls that became part classroom and part gentle reminder of the fragility of the natural world. Far below the tender quiet of the trails that Colin and his mother were experiencing, in the valley, a ski resort grew along with further development that included the building of a golf course on the same ground where decades before cars for the 1960 Winter Olympics had parked. Numerous other mountain towns with ski areas throughout the country experience the same penchant for growth and development. What happened in Olympic Valley felt both inevitable—and, to Colin's way of thinking, tragic.

Colin eventually moved away from the valley he had loved for a number of reasons that were intensely personal. He had mentioned to his brother many times that perhaps the hardest thing with growing older was reconciling what you remembered, which no longer was, with what was happening now, which wasn't worth remembering at all. He told Brad that the only way he would ever move back to Lake Tahoe was if he ever met someone special. Otherwise, the memories of what once was were too hard to bear.

Emily, in her early 30s then, grew up in Northern California's Sonoma County. She played piano as a young girl, danced, and sang in the choir. There were also visits to Lake Tahoe. She fell in love with the place immediately. "Lake Tahoe has always been my special place," she said. "I love being there so much. It's a place where there is so much life, so much natural wonder to it." They met thanks to the connection of Emily's landlord, who happened to be Colin's brother. Their connection was rooted in their common interest of Lake Tahoe: Emily's love of it, and Colin's awareness of how it forged so much of how he viewed the world around him.

"It was pretty clear that was the connection," Colin said. "We both love being up in the mountains and being on the trails. Our love of the trails, and the mountains . . . that was a great way to get a relationship started."

Their first date was a hike up Shirley Canyon, a place that Colin knew well. He had written about the area quite movingly in his 1995 *Audubon Magazine* article, "A Place Worth Fighting For," which was a an award-winning story. As a precociously curious young boy, he had first experienced the hike with his mother, who, at the time was the woman he most loved. Now he was experiencing it again with the woman he was about to love.

"It was the best date ever," Emily said. "I loved that hike. I loved being with Colin. He shared so much as we made that hike together. I discovered what a sensitive and caring person Colin was, and how he could put these wonderful thoughts together and describe things so well. The wilderness has always affected me in a really profound way. As I was experiencing that hike with Colin, I was having those same kinds of feelings. He was putting into words how the wilderness has always affected me."

They were married in 2013 at Lake Tahoe's Baldwin Beach, a place that meant so much to Emily. Her family had kept a cabin on Tahoe's south shore, not far from the beach where the cinnamon-colored sand might be the softest and most forgiving of any of the beaches in and around the 78 miles of Lake Tahoe. Emily wore a vintage wedding dress with running shoes. You couldn't have found a more appropriately dressed bride wearing two of the symbols she most loved in her life: a dress that spoke to her vows to a special man who shared her love of the wilderness, and shoes that spoke to her dexterous, light, and lovely way she moved whenever she was on a trail.

Finding a Fragile Peace

Emily's relationship with running had always been complicated. By 14, she was running as a member of the varsity cross-country team at Petaluma High School in Sonoma County. There were lofty expectations for athletic excellence. She seemed well on her way to becoming a star high school cross country runner for the Trojans. It was just one of many activities that Emily excelled at. She was a member of the Future Farmers of America. Her love of animals and the natural world had been rewarded with numerous prizes and commendations. She was also an artist, and the cabin that her family kept at South Lake Tahoe often captured her imagination as she sketched the trees of nearby Fallen Leaf Lake, of the mountains that rose above the south shore signaling an enticing entrance into the High Sierra. Her youthful accomplishments, though, gave way to a different sort of reality. Over the next few years, Emily would battle anorexia. At one point, her weight dropped to 62 pounds. For more than a year, she lived in a treatment facility. At first, she did not cooperate with the counselors and medical professionals at the treatment facility. She chose not to speak at all. She remained mute for months. She remembered choosing to retreat behind her long blonde hair and not interact in any meaningful way with anyone. Eventually, after about six months, she did accept treatment. She attended college at Humboldt State University and then went to massage therapy school in Colorado.

It took years of starts and stops, of wondering what her relationship with running needed to be while also working on her psychological mindset and building her body back to the point where it could withstand the rigors of training. Her parents were always cautioning her about her running. They worried that maybe she was doing too much, too soon.

Colin, as he came to know her, realized that Emily wanted to run because it was a vehicle for her to explore and experience what she truly enjoyed in life: the beauty of nature. Every time they would share the trails together, first hiking and eventually Emily running and Colin on his mountain bike, he could see that she was a person whose perception and senses were unlike any other he'd ever met in his life. He had always been an observant person himself; a keen listener, he never interrupts, always letting the other person finish their thought or their sentence before he begins. And yet, the more time Colin was with Emily on trails, the more he felt he was seeing some things for the very first time. Whatever changes he had made in his relationship with Lake Tahoe were because of her. She was the one who had helped him rediscover pieces of the little boy who had spent so many happy and contented hours in the mountains above Olympic Valley.

"I don't know how many rocks she finds that are in a shape of a heart on the trail, but it's a lot, much more than you or I would even notice," Colin said. "Emily has this special type of relationship with the trail that goes pretty deep. Whenever I'm with her outdoors, I'm just blown away by the beauty that she is always able to discover. And to be able to run while doing that? That's as good as it can get."

So it shouldn't have come as too great of a surprise that when Emily turned to racing ultra running, she found almost immediate success. Her first 50-mile and 100-mile races came within about a month of each other at another picturesque mountain spot, Leadville, Colorado, in 2012. In 2014, she placed ninth at the Ultra Tour du Mont Blanc (UTMB) race, a 104-mile race that starts on a Friday night in late August in the mountain sports mecca of Chamonix, France. This race features a field of a couple thousand runners from all over the world, takes them through France, Italy, and Switzerland and features more than 30,000 feet of climbing. UTMB is as tortuous as it is beautiful. Only a handful of Americans have ever won or placed in the top 10 there. It was during her UTMB race that Emily, who will tell you she is the person who always been hardest on herself, received a text message from her father (among many other friends and family) that acknowledged she was where she needed to be: running. Running in one of the world's most beautiful and challenging races.

"This is something that I love," she said of running trails. "It inspires me and makes me happy. It's part of who I am. Everything I attempt in my life, I put my heart into it. Sometimes I can be too serious or too hard on myself. It's those moments where I'm being too hard on myself where I do try to smile, to feel, and remind myself of why I'm running in the first place. You can know the bends and climbs of the trails you run by heart, but they are always morphing into a new beauty with each passing season. I love observing and feeling the changes, until the rhythm of the earth becomes my own. It's a comforting reminder of the impermanence of all things. I seek solace and challenge on these trails, especially when you need to find a fragile peace."

More than a few times since he's known Emily, Colin has found himself slowing down instead of speeding up. He will be riding his mountain bike and spot a rock. Years ago he would've blown right by it. Because of Emily, he stops, goes eye-level to the ground sometimes, and inspects the rocks. It is amazing how many of the rocks on a trail, if you find the time to slow down and look closely enough, resemble a heart. It's a window in time. Colin often thinks of the rocks he finds, sometimes putting them in his pocket so he can bring them home and show them to his wife. The rocks are a reminder that for Emily, trails can be used to race over, certainly. But more importantly, the trails she runs on possess life and experiences all of their own. Every rock has a story. Every life has meaning. Everything that Emily has done in her life, whether working through the pain of her early years or simply going out for a run in her late 30s and into her 40s, has been about finding peace in the beauty of her surroundings.

"Being in nature can bring us back to the moment and provide healing," Emily said. "I've often stood in awe, feeling the simplicity, the grandeur, and miracles of flowers and mountains. It has been an essential and influential practice for me for most of my life. Some days I'd realize that my pace was too quick. To fully experience a oneness with nature, I'd have to sit quietly and observe. My mind would stop working on problems and instead, I'd listen and look."

There Are No Strangers

After a 10-year hiatus from running Western States, I returned as a runner to the event I love more than any other in 2021. It was a tortuous day, with temperatures rising into the low 100s. I ran conservatively, hunkering down near the back quarter of the race's 369 runners for most of the day and through a very warm night. The final six miles, my pacer, Lauren Watson, and I reflected on what had been a sort of epic journey where the Western States runners were heroes and heroines in their own mini-drama of heat, of suffering, of wanting not to go on but then pushing forward anyway because we all entered the race in the hope of achieving the simple dream of successfully running 100.2 miles. The journey was a reminder of how we needed to be aware of our limitations even as we were in the midst of boldly working to achieve a dream. As we entered the Robie Point neighborhood that signals only about a mile to go to the finish, there were flags, banners, handwritten signs, and an expectant electricity that made the entire neighborhood feel like it was in the middle of a Fourth of July street party. Garden hoses to douse us were plentiful, as were the dozens of rows of people sitting in lawn chairs. When the people in the lawn chairs would see us, they would rise out of their chairs and start cheering wildly.

"Only a mile to go!"

"You've got this!"

"Look at that smile! Keep smiling!"

"Way to get it done!"

There are never any strangers in this Robie Point neighborhood when Western States is being run. Only friends. Only heroines and heroes who have traveled a great distance, against great odds, who have written their own fable for the previous 99 miles. The Robie Point neighborhood people realize this better than anyone. They exhibited pure, unconditional love in the praise they heaped on us from their shaded driveways and their front porches. Their words lifted me. Their words lifted all of us, a love letter exchanged between perfect strangers that bonded us together in what felt like a moment that I hoped would never end. It was hard not to get carried away with it all. I couldn't help myself. I began blowing kisses to them and told them that I loved them, too, each and every one of them, for coming out and believing in all of us.

Lauren and I started to run downhill from the neighborhood, with friends from our running group seemingly appearing out of nowhere to join us for the run to the Placer High School track and the finish line. It was then that I saw Emily. She was standing to the side of our caravan but beaming. I reached out and hugged her. She congratulated me for a great run. I motioned to her.

"Come on!" I yelled. "You need to run with us to the finish, Emily! Come on!"

Colin was standing nearby with their precious kindergarten-aged daughter, Aila. Emily looked to Colin to see if it was OK. He gave her permission with a smiling thumbs-up. Colin has always possessed the most amazing smile. As a clinical social worker and therapist, I'm sure his clients feel a sense of reassurance and understanding whenever they are with him. As he waved to me, with Emily joining us for the final mile, I was thankful to him. Like all of us, he has always known how wondrous it is whenever his wife runs free. We headed down Robie Point back into the more traditional neighborhoods, where you feel the pressures of having run nearly 100 miles through infernal canyons and far-off stretches of rocky ridgeline begin to lift. We swooped down over what the Western States runners often call "the white bridge," which signals about a half mile to go to the finish, toward the welcoming sound of public address announcer "Tropical" John Medinger's low baritone of a voice reading off the names and sharing a few lines of story about each runner crossing the finish line. I've run 100 miles before, several times in my life, but I can't recall a moment quite like the moment I was experiencing. I was aware of my achievement and knew that soon Tropical John would be reading off my name as I hit the track for my finish. But I also had so many other thoughts in my head, thoughts I don't normally have at the end of a 100-mile race. My friends and family who were running alongside me, laughing and cheering, were primarily on my mind. I also thought about Emily running next to me and how honored I felt to have her company as well. There were so many others who had started this journey with me more than 29 hours earlier at 5 a.m. in Olympic Valley. For a variety of reasons, not all of them had made it to that point. To be able to finish with a person I admired for her quiet tenacity throughout a number of challenges in her life made the moment feel all the more powerful. Emily and Colin, in fact, had been through a lot over the past several years. Aila's birth was without a doubt a huge joy to the couple. The little girl with the wide, expressive blue eyes looks very much like her mother and possesses the same ability to make an instant connection with everyone she meets. She is one of those types of children who seem to understand that it's not all about them, that whenever you experience something with someone else, the intrinsic joy is actually doubled. Giving birth also brought with it a struggle to completely heal, with a litany of postpartum injuries that kept Emily from returning to the same high level of accomplishment she had experienced at UTMB and several other races prior to her pregnancy. Throughout it all, Emily found solace in the fact that even if there were injuries, it didn't mean her life was meant to stop. "Sometimes the universe tells you to sit still," she said. "There could not have been a more appropriate time, as I've marveled each day by how quickly Aila is growing and changing and showing us more and more the tender and bright spirit she is."

Battling her own injuries and finding a sense of a new normal as a new mother was one thing for Emily, but her family's challenges didn't end there. Colin was in the backcountry skiing in April 2018 when he was involved in an avalanche. The trauma was such that his upper body filled with blood clots, nearly costing him his life in the days afterward. One of his legs was shattered, with the tendon that attached his hamstring to the pelvis ripped from the bone. In June of 2018, the tendon was reattached, though Colin remained on crutches for most of the rest of the year.

All of it—giving birth, the injuries, Colin's terrible mishap in the backcountry, working long hours as an intensive cardiac rehabilitation nurse at Renown Medical Center before and during the pandemic—might have been enough for most people to simply give in and give up on running. What was the point? Where was the soothing, silent music that Emily had always experienced whenever she was on the trails? We know that the life of the mind and the body can often become one, but only when both are flowing steadily toward a common goal in harmony with one another does this usually happen. It is a sinewy and synaptic marriage that sometimes, if we are incredibly lucky, can last a lifetime. More often, though, the synchronous sense of the mind and the body flowing as one can be fleeting. Instead of a lifetime, this destination can turn into a cruel cul-de-sac. Instead of lasting for all of your days, this flow can taunt and be brief. It can be for a single season, or even less than that. Somehow, perhaps because of the spaciousness of her heart, Emily had found a path through the very challenges that had confronted her. Maybe, like the heart rocks she and Colin shared with one another, her own heart was simply too large to allow her to fully stop in her tracks. There had been psychological and physical pain, but she had always kept moving. If there is any value in running great distances, maybe that's the most important thing that we learn: If you stop, there is no chance that you will ever finish.

And that was what I felt as Emily ran next to me and my family as we made our way onto the Placer High School track. I could feel her generosity and could see as she ran along next to me, her face alight with our movement, that she possesses an ability to rise, to go inside herself as she experiences the triumphs and successes of others, to live a life at a great, empathetic altitude. It also wasn't lost on me at that moment that throughout her ultra-running career, she had always wished to run Western States. Emily had the opportunity at a certain juncture in her athletic career to become one of the greatest ultra runners of her time. The prospect of having something that valuable in your grasp could be intoxicating. Yet that had never been the destination Emily was seeking. Athletic achievement can reaffirm everything we have ever thought about ourselves, which certainly can be a good thing. But it can also be limiting. I was in the final 18 minutes of the race before it would end at the 30-hour cutoff. This might not have been the finish line that Emily had always dreamed about when she dreamed of Western States. But her presence with us, how engrossed she was in the moment as she ran along with us, made it feel right. This wasn't a podium finish. This was life. Emily's life had come to be about so much more than running.

I felt all of this as I crossed the finish line with a loud whoop, hugs, and tears with my friends and family. Not long after, Emily and Colin and Aila were there. I could see Emily had tears in her eyes, too. Aila stepped forward and grabbed me around my waist, giving me a spontaneous hug that only a small child who sees only beauty in the world can do. I looked down at this precious little girl who possesses the same blue eyes worn smooth by the wonders of life and hugged her back tightly. This was a family I now felt a part of. This was a family that through all of the tests of the preceding few years had come to understand that life isn't about accomplishment or acquisition or accolades. It is about the miracle of slowing down, of understanding the sheer comfort that can come when you let the world around you slowly and intentionally sink into your soul.

Years before, when Emily had seemingly come out of nowhere to win Silver State, we hadn't known who she was. Knowing Emily in the years since has taught me that the world, for all of its tragedy, challenges, and frustrations, also has a heart-shaped beauty to it. More than anything when you see the world as she does, this heart-shaped beauty becomes like a reddening sunset. At the end of each day, such natural beauty always challenges your senses. And your reaction, when you've done the things that Emily Richards has done and is still yet to do, is that you wish to go out again, into the next morning and into the next day, and hear yet again the mysteries of life whispering gently to you, along the trails that you will always run.

CHAPTER 6

Team **Watson**

Sometimes, in running and in life, you come close to losing some-one or something in a way that makes you stop and reconsider your priorities. When that someone happens to be not only a lovely person but also an integral part of your team, it's an even tougher realization that you need to take to heart.

Lauren Watson is one of those rare people who are known in the sports world as a "glue" person. Because of who she is and how she possesses an innate sense of caring for others in her soul, she holds people and groups together. We didn't know any of this about her, however, on a fateful evening several years ago when Lauren came out to one of our group runs. It was a reminder to us all that you had better make sure that at the end of every group trail run you ever hold, that all of the runners who show up at the beginning are accounted for in the end. If you don't, the lives of dozens of trail runners might not ever be the same again.

The Schedule

Our "group," as it were, has been holding group runs every Tuesday and Thursday night for the better part of two decades now. The runs are usually on trails, are held in the early evening at 5:45 p.m., and feature anywhere from two runners to about 20. Depending on the time of year and what races are looming on the upcoming northern California/northern Nevada ultra calendar, the weeknight runs can vary anywhere from about six miles to about 10 miles. The runs were the brainchild of northern Nevada's godfather, Roland Martin. Roland's idea was grounded in strict accountability. No matter what kind of day you might have had at work, no matter how tired you might have been, no matter what other responsibilities you might have in terms of one's family and friends, every Tuesday and Thursday night was sacro-sanct. If there was snow on the ground, you ran. If the wind whipped through one of the many old Reno ranches that had been converted into regional open space and parks, like Bartley Ranch and its small-ish carveout pasture situated below a rocky promontory overlooking Reno called "Windy Hill," you tucked your chin down and, like a deckhand duty-bound to hold their ground on a sailboat rollicked by unruly seas, you leaned into the wind and didn't give into it. If there were nights in the summer when the temperatures were still hovering uncomfortably in the mid-90s, you stared the heat down and fought the temptation to retreat into your home's air conditioning and you ran, even as your body's internal radiator felt like it was about to blow. There was also the matter of the "Schedule." The Schedule became our Bible, especially if you were training for a hundred-miler. It was written out in Roland's careful and lawyerly longhand, often in capi-tal letters for emphasis. Each month contained different workouts and different distances, shorter runs early in the year, then building grad-ually over the next few months in duration and length. The Schedule had a sort of mythic quality to it. There were stories from years earlier of the runners who had followed Roland's training schedule and then successfully found their finish lines. Roland's good friend, Robert Sobsey, was one of the first local runners to finish Western States more than once, finishing the race five times in the space of 12 years from 1983-1995. Robert recalled years later that one of those early years he ran in honor of his twin brother, Roger, who died unexpectedly in 1987. As he ran around the track at Placer High School that year, the public address announcer mentioned the fact that Robert was running that year for his late brother. Robert burst into tears as he covered the final few yards, moved by the memory of his brother, who had also been a runner, and also moved by the fact that all of those runs on Roland's schedule had helped pave his way to that emotional moment. As the Schedule morphed from longhand legal-pad versions to PDFs that were circulated like cryptocurrency, as a kind of possession that was incredibly valued yet impossible to accurately place a value upon, it became in my mind the emotional equivalent to what the Sumerians had first invented during the Bronze Age. The first calendars were a means for civilization to schedule progress. The Schedule, I've always felt, has been about something more: the day-by-day, week-by-week, month-by-month process of building toward a seemingly far-off goal, as well as the potential for personal reinvention, where we become obsessed with those times in our life when we travel to the edge of what we had previously thought was possible. Our sensitivities become less inhibited. The impossible becomes somewhat possible, or at least relatable to the small universe of the other runners you meet every Tuesday and Thursday night. That, to me, was always the essence of the Schedule. It wasn't Roland's specific workouts that actually mattered. But their insistency on consistency, on "the value of always showing up," as one of Roland's best friends and apostles, Lon Monroe, put it so succinctly after one of those cold, wet, and muddy nights where we shivered together at a trail-head following a particular bone-chilling weeknight's run, was always at the Schedule's forefront. It was the subtext that was more important to me. It was the potential to grow emotionally as well as physically that always seemed to matter more.

Nowhere was this more apparent than the night we almost lost Lauren before we even had a chance to know who she was. Lauren Watson was 30 years old in the fall of 2015. She was fresh off having completed her first two ultras ever, the American Canyon 50K in February and then the Sierra Crest 50K near Donner Pass in August. She had run Sierra Crest with her dad, Bill, and came out to one of our weeknight runs out of curiosity more than anything else. I remember her being exceptionally bright and attentive, her blue eyes fastened carefully to each person who spoke. You always figure that when some-one pays that close attention to whatever is being said, particularly as instructions are given on where to go, the odds of getting lost on a trail run should be greatly diminished. Not that night. We were making our way along a rutted and rocky route full of sagebrush and thorns and prickly branches known as the Meat Grinder, located in the hills west of Reno. At one point, you pass through an undeveloped development that the Great Recession of 2009 effectively killed off, running by a ghost yard of never-used pads of concrete foundations and paved driveways that never had a homeowner's car drive over them at the end of a long workday. Lauren and another new runner, Lacey Frerking, disappeared on us somewhere through the dead development. As we dropped down to a trailhead, Lauren and the other new runner were nowhere to be found until they suddenly appeared, high above the trailhead on a dirt road that led from one of the unused driveways. We called to them. They called back down to us.

"Sorry!" they yelled.

In a few minutes, we were all reunited, and the run continued on.

It would have been easy for Lauren to disappear after that run. Joining a running group, even one like ours, which I affectionately refer to as "The Island of Misfit Toys" for the wide range of abilities and backgrounds that we all represent, sometimes can be a little daunting. But Lauren wasn't afraid at all. She engaged everyone in meaningful conversation. She remembered everyone's name. She had an affinity for complex thought, which, given her background as a chemist, shouldn't have been too surprising. And she was curious. Extremely curious and unafraid to ask questions. A few months later, as I got to know her better and as I was introduced to her husband, Jimmy, I came to discover that Lauren was a person who was never careless with her feelings and was always thoughtful in considering how her feelings might affect the people she knew. There was a four-mile cross-country race we ran that late fall, she and Jimmy and I, that took us across the former site of the Ballardini Ranch, one of many working ranches in the foothills of Reno that had been lost to time, the pastures turned to the rooftops of housing developments. I carried on, as I usually do, for several minutes about Ballardini Ranch's history. Lauren listened carefully to everything I was saying. We ran the race that day, then ran back to our cars, and I thought nothing more of it. Then a few weeks later, when on a weeknight run, Lauren began to pepper me with questions about Ballardini Ranch. She had listened to everything I had said. Her capacity to remember the salient details from any conversation she had was impressive. A year or so after I met Lauren, I happened to be interviewing one of our university's top young chemistry professors. The professor wasn't much older than Lauren was. He wore glasses and had facial hair that dangled off his chin almost as an afterthought. Lauren had been one of the professor's students and had worked in his lab when she was an undergraduate. When I mentioned her name and that I often ran with her, his face lit up. "You remember her?" I asked. "Of course," the professor said. "You don't forget a student like Lauren. In a lab situation, you always need the students who are kind of like 'the glue' for the other students. They're the ones who take a sincere interest in the other students. That's the way Lauren was in our lab."

She and Jimmy quickly became part of the supportive underpinning of the Silver State Striders, our trail running club. If someone needed a pacer or someone to crew for them, Lauren and Jimmy were always first in line to help.

Seeing Beauty in the Challenges

We met on a cool night in early April 2019, the five of us—Lauren, Jimmy, Annie, Katie, and I—for a run. Jimmy was by then readying for a months-long cancer treatment path that would hopefully end in happiness and success. Lauren was readying herself to be by her husband's side, every step of the way. It was one of those strange moments in life where you realize that the coming months would be anything but normal, and the first instinct is to seek out the comfort of the familiar. For all of us, the familiar, the safe, the already explored, meant a run. We ran into Evans Canyon from Rancho San Rafael Park, covering the first few miles of the Silver State 50 course. We chatted, we laughed, we shared moments of silence, we ran together, as a group of friends always does—for a while one of us would lead, then another, our conversation drifting from the pleasant present to the future, which interestingly enough began to drift to what we had first not wanted to talk about at all. Our trail conversation seemed to focus more as the miles passed by on what was still ahead of us. At one point, I let Jimmy, Lauren, Annie, and Katie all pull ahead of me and watched the four of them running together. Against the blunt orange hills of Peavine and following in the tracks of coyotes, they were like the early evening we were running through that night—full of raw, spirited energy, in complete harmony with the world around them.

For that moment, it was easy to forget the cancer treatment for Jimmy or an upcoming procedure on my knee for me. Our run that night was more about the things that had come to inform all of our existences over the past several years. Races run and races still to come. Hundred-mile debuts and hundred-mile finishes. Every act we have as runners is often an act of creation. For every memory we create, there are hundreds of hours of running and training and moments where our imaginations carry us to the races we have yet to run. The wonder is in the distances we cover; the mystic necessity and value of it all comes after we run those prodigious distances and then begin plotting anew. We said our goodbyes that night, a spring night that felt transcendent and tender, as so many spring nights feel in northern Nevada, knowing full well that although there was a chance things might not ever be the same, somehow, they would still be all right. This is one of the underlying themes in Jimmy and Lauren's life. Even when faced with a challenge, even if the challenge is intensely real, the two of them know there is always beauty and value that can come of it.

I saw that play out about a month later, at the Quicksilver 100K at Almaden Quicksilver County Park. There are a couple of points of preamble here before I get to what transpired. Quicksilver has a long history. It dates back to the early 1980s, first as a 50-miler, and today as a 100K. It is run on one of the most diverse and brutal courses in all of northern California. The minute you start running, you immediately step back into a time when the area was home to the second largest mercury (quicksilver) mine on the face of the planet. Before the mines, the native Ohlone people made the area their home, walking through a place where they found harmony and life. There are old trestles and chimneys and tramways and an old cemetery that you circle in the early miles of the race, still under headlamp, reminding you of what has been. Tree-studded grass hills roll and wind in an unrelenting fashion. There are, more or less, about 13,000 feet of climbing and a few sections where you are doing nothing but either running straight up or going straight down. The course is terribly unforgiving and requires constant concentration and focus. Whenever I've run Quicksilver, I can't help but think of the words of the writer Mary Austin. She wasn't writing of Quicksilver, but of Death Valley, and her words do a movingly eloquent job of describing the push-pull, love-hate, and hard-fought beauty of its challenge, ". . . the loneliest land that ever came out of God's hands . . . one that lays such a hold on the affections." Quicksilver asks a lot of you. It makes your legs heavy, and the exposed heat tilts your vision. The breathless calm of its humid trails and tree-lined hills that smell like deep, dry earth and somehow never offer enough shade are a constant reminder that you need to be careful when you run there. Fanciful dreams of getting a Western States qualifier can quickly turn into a devil's dance if you are not wise.

And that was what Lauren was after. Her Western States quali-fier and her ticket into that December's Western States lottery, gained through the wisdom of letting go of all obstacles and simply running in the calm embrace of knowing you have it within you to go the distance. Jimmy was at home for Quicksilver weekend, on the road to more treatment. Lauren's goal was simple. She would enlist the ebullient presence and take-charge teacher's personality of a good friend of all of us, Kaycee Green, for a quick trip to Quicksilver, nab a Western States qualifier, then head right home to be with Jimmy. The entire process, if Lauren played her cards right, would take a little more than 30 hours, from doorstep to Quicksilver and back to doorstep.

The day was long and challenging, yet Lauren never wavered. At the early aid stations, she smiled and asked how Annie and Katie were running. Her focus seemed to be on the mile at hand, and with Kaycee's constant encouragement, her face was always bright with the possibility of what was still ahead. In one of those moments that truly come to define the value of friendship, Kaycee, nursing an injured hip, jumped in and paced her friend over the final half of the race. Quicksilver offers few concessions to its runners, one of them being that the race finishes on a long (but of course, brutal) downhill. Runners swoop down into the finish near Quicksilver Park's Mockingbird entrance to the whoops and howls and cheers of the organizers, to the high fives and hugs of their friends and families. Watching runners finish down that steep hill is a lot like watching people in a water park heading headlong down one of those incredibly steep slides. You know things will probably turn out all right as long as the runner maintains his or her balance on the out-of-control cannonball run to the finish.

I will always remember Lauren's finish. If there is a way to bottle an expression of a runner wearing her blue Strider hat on backwards who has accomplished her goal of the day, under the greatest of pressure and showing the greatest of grace, I'd want to bottle what I saw as Jill and I stood near the finish. The air was finally beginning to cool, the shadows growing longer, the unrelenting, sharp stare of day finally starting to give way to the soft May music of early night. You could hear the night birds beginning to chirp and smell Quicksilver's world-class, all-you-can-eat barbecue lazily wafting through the air nearby.

Lauren had given a lot that day. With the blessing of her husband, she'd gone out to seek something important. This would be her only chance to bag a Western States qualifier in 2019, given the schedule of Jimmy's treatments and recovery that were still to come. But it was more that made the moment special. Lauren's journey to Quicksilver that weekend had staked out a defiant sort of independent metaphoric space where we all seek to find our limits and make a map of where we were before running a race, and where we land after. Cancer had entered Jimmy's and Lauren's lives. But they weren't about to let it end their lives.

Lauren's smile as she ran down that landslide of trail to the finish was like a painting of all of our collective experience. There were places she had known didn't exist before she had run, and, nearing the finish, smiling, she had found some of them to carry back with her to Jimmy and to the life that they would share ahead. For Lauren, that experience at Quicksilver was one that I think has truly defined her. It was a reminder of how a race that seemingly can be so brutal and difficult somehow always reminds us how much we can find in ourselves to love.

Hoping for Better Days on the Horizon

Jimmy's cancer treatments were not easy. From the day he was diagnosed with testicular cancer on April 4, 2019, Jimmy's life was a reminder of how quickly things can change. He read Psalm 46 as he had headed into surgery, and he kept the words on his mind as he went through treatment.

"God is our refuge and strength/an ever-present help in trouble/ Therefore we will not fear, though the earth give way/and the mountains fall into the heart of the sea/though its waters roar and foam/ and the mountains quake with their surging/There is a river whose streams make/glad the city of God/the holy place where the Most High dwells."

There was another surgery to implant a port in his chest to help with the transfusion of the chemotherapy drugs he would receive. Jimmy felt in a way that at 32, his life had come full circle. His surgery was at the oldest hospital in Reno, St. Mary's, where he had also been born. He was born a preemie, arriving too early at 28 weeks. As a newborn, Jimmy spent his first few weeks in an incubator at St. Mary's. "They had to heat me up so they could bring me home," Jimmy had always joked about his parents' first responsibility to him. He had fought for his life as a baby, and now he was back at St. Mary's, fighting again. There were just as many uncertainties in May 2019 as there had been in 1986 when he was born. But Jimmy was confident and optimistic. He relied on his faith— his faith in a higher power plus the faith that Lauren and his parents had in him that he possessed an uncommonly deep reservoir of fortitude and courage. He didn't want to let them down. He was also aware that cancer, as he embarked on the journey to fight it, would always be a part of his life going forward. The thought didn't scare him or somehow make him feel that he needed to hide it. It didn't define him as much as it reminded him that we must constantly be aware that life is precious and that, if at all possible, we must make the most of it while we have it. "I'm not sure why cancer is part of my story," he said. "But it is. The thing I'm most thankful about is the overwhelming amount of love, support, and prayers we've received from everyone we know. It's meant a lot to me."

Jimmy spent more than 100 hours in one of the chairs at the brick-walled Cancer Care Specialists building in Reno receiving chemotherapy. His long and unruly red hair fell out. He lost weight. He took on water and gained weight. His energy level would ebb. He suffered terrible heartburn. There was constipation, and neuropathy in his hands and feet. His fingernails became brittle. He was constantly tasting metal in his mouth. He was always achy, always feeling as if he were in a fog. "Chemo brain," he called it. Each cycle was a stretch of five days straight of chemotherapy, all starting at 8 a.m., six to seven hours per day. Throughout it all, Jimmy tried to stay focused. "I felt that with every (chemotherapy) bag done, I was one step closer to the finish line," he said. "I needed to remind myself that there always needs to be better days on the horizon."

And of course Jimmy did something more. He was a cancer patient who worried about other cancer patients. As he received his treatment, it was hard not to be moved by those who were doing the same at Cancer Care Specialists. They were old and young. They were in far worse and in far better shape than Jimmy. Some had a wife like Lauren who was always there, and some did not. Their experiences, their expected outcomes, and their lives, what was left and what was yet to come, infiltrated Jimmy's consciousness the same way the needs, wants, and desires of those he rode dirt bikes with, or ran with had. He was learning that cancer often doesn't follow the rules, and often a cancer patient's biggest challenge isn't necessarily the disease (though it is truly formidable), but rather a patient's fight to maintain their identity in a world that is completely turned upside down by the diagnosis and the treatment that follows. He was finding that the best way forward was highly personal. He had seen how cancer patients could be so different in how they dealt with the moment, what the treatments were doing to them physically, and how they looked to the possibilities of the future when their treatments had ended and their "normal" lives were ready to resume. Some of them could be a like a painter who loses their sense of color and then without hesitation simply pivots to working in black and white. Their adaptability was simply uncanny to him. There was the inherent uncertainty for others, a fear of being too flexible or adjusting too well to the circumstances that inhibited their chances for recovery, for moving forward once treatment had ended. Jimmy was never one to feel like he had all the answers. He was too humble a soul to feel that way. But as Jimmy went through the draining and painful process of chemotherapy, he came to realize that the process had shaped his understanding of his illness and that maybe he could help others come to understand what it meant as well. So he became a contributor at Elly Health, an audio app designed to help cancer patients as they face the disease. He wanted to share with other cancer patients the idea that, as he put it so well, "Cancer's part of my story, but that's not the whole book."

He knew cancer wasn't the whole story because of the reminders of what his life had once been like and what it needed to be like again. For his birthday, Lauren bought him a pair of running shoes. Jimmy had just finished his final round of chemotherapy and hadn't been doing any running at all. He tried the shoes on. But he was too weak and wobbly to run in them. Lauren, always patient, smiled. "It's OK," she told her husband. "You'll be back." Jimmy felt terrible that he wasn't strong enough to run yet. But Lauren reassured him. "You'll be back," she said again, as confident as Jimmy was unsure. But then he remembered why Lauren was so certain he would come back. She had always been the person in his life who had brought so much life to everything. She'd been the "glue" in her chemistry laboratory; she'd been the person who had become the "connector" at all of the Strider weeknight runs, gathering names and information about any of the new runners who showed up, making sure that the lead group never ran so far ahead of the new runners that the new runners ever became lost or grew discouraged; she'd been the person who'd sat there quietly by his side during his chemo; she'd been the person who would share inspirational sayings and verses with Jimmy to get him through the difficult moments, like the "Verse of the Week" that welcomed him one morning on a small chalkboard in their home: "Let us Run with ENDURANCE the Race God has set before us (Hebrews 12:1)."

And it all worked. Jimmy did come back.

Be Here Today

Jimmy was deemed cancer-free by August 17, 2019. In October, Jimmy and Lauren celebrated their 10th wedding anniversary by riding their Honda dirt bikes up and down the Baja Peninsula. They spent time with their rescue dogs, Ollie and Ivan. The pandemic hit in 2020, and the Watsons hunkered down like all of the rest of us. Jimmy's work as a graphic designer for the Bonanza Casino in Reno went away for a few months, then returned. Lauren's work in the Nevada State Health Laboratory as a chemist put her on the frontlines of understanding why COVID-19 was posing such a threat to the country. Still, there were moments where things almost felt normal. Jimmy supported and crewed a friend on the 514-mile Vegas-to-Reno dirt bike race in mid-August 2020. Lauren completed her first hundred-miler ever on a portion of the historic Pony Express Trail in Utah, the Pony Express Trail 100 Mile Endurance Run, in under 24 hours. In April 2021, Jimmy paced another good friend, Heidy Siwajian, to a finish at the Zion 100K in Utah. It took Heidy, who is a spirited and talkative young woman, about 21 hours to finish. There were points where Heidy really struggled, turning frequent cursing into flat-out bouts of crying. It was dark, cold, and the Zion slickrock was its usual unforgiving and obstinate obstruction to moving with any type of efficiency. Yet Jimmy remained steadfast. He kept offering Heidy words of encouragement, even as she grew increasingly more frustrated and forlorn. "You can do it, Heidy," Jimmy kept reassuring her. Afterward, Heidy told Jimmy, "You had no way of knowing what you were signing up for, but you were the calm to my storm. You believed in me more than I believed in myself, and your faith in me carried me through that final 20 miles. I felt like a chaotic bowling ball, but I had you as my bumper lane, very literally at times as you made sure I didn't fall off the mesa. One thing is for sure. I wouldn't have made it without you."

In October 2021, the Watsons returned to Quicksilver. The race is usually held each May, but due to the pandemic, the event shifted to the fall. Lauren paced the Watson's physical trainer and friend, Miles Brazil, in the 100K and Jimmy ran his first ultra since his cancer diagnosis by running the 50K. I entered the 50K as well. It was my goal to run the entire distance with Jimmy. As we ran together on a day that was surprisingly mild by Quicksilver standards, with temperatures in the mid-60s, it became apparent to me that Jimmy was a different runner than the one I remembered from before his cancer diagnosis in 2019. He and Lauren had been making regular visits to Miles' gym, working on strength training and flexibility. Jimmy's tall and lanky frame had become more muscular. He had certainly filled out since some of the hard days of chemo treatment, and what was obvious to me was how confidently he was running, powered by a new-found strength that had come about through hours in a gym and perhaps through hours of coming to understand that his cancer, as he had put it so well, had been a "piece of my life, but it hasn't been my whole story." A few months earlier, in August 2021, crewed by Lauren and his friends and family, this new strength was evident when Jimmy had finished the 489-mile Vegas-to-Reno dirt bike race himself. It had been a longtime goal, one that had to be put on the shelf with Jimmy's cancer diagnosis and the pandemic. We all drove out to the Vegas-to-Reno finish line that incredible night, the finish line not far from the small town of Dayton, Nevada, which not that many years before had seen herds of sheep tended by Basque sheepherders often run down its main street. Jimmy had experienced life all in a day that day as he used dirt bike skills he had honed since he was a boy. He remembered later that as he sped through a remote valley the sun's rays burst through the cloud cover for a moment, a light so brilliant and pure that it took his breath away. There was only horizon ahead. He remembered what his grandmother always told him—that the sun rays were always a sign of God's love shining down on you. When he finished at the Dayton Fairgrounds, just as the sun was going down, Jimmy told the announcer at finish that he had been diagnosed with testicular cancer in 2019 and if not for Lauren, his friends and family, his doctors, and a whole host of people who had prayed for him, he probably wouldn't have been standing at there at all, covered in dust, his face sunburned from the August heat. But Jimmy said to our chorus of cheers, "I'm here today, and I just finished Vegas to Reno."

And as we ran together on that October day at Quicksilver a couple of months later, Jimmy's effort was constant and strong. I remembered how his wife had come here in spring 2019 to get her Western States qualifier, and Jimmy was at home, thinking of the wife he had met at a college inter-varsity faith meeting while they were students at the University of Nevada, Reno. There was so much uncertainty to what their futures held as Lauren raced Quicksilver and Jimmy was undergoing treatment. Now it was his turn. He was racing Quicksilver with undaunted and joyful courage. And then over the final miles of Jimmy's first ultra since his cancer diagnosis, he began a sustained surge for the finish line. I tried to keep pace, but I couldn't. Jimmy was just too strong. I've run with too many runners over the years to even remember, but I do know that instance with Jimmy was a moment I was never going to forget. Jimmy had always said that what got him through his cancer treatment was always knowing that there was a finish line he was going to reach. Every day, every round of chemo, and every procedure had been about reaching a finish line. On this day, Jimmy reached the Quicksilver finish line about two strides ahead of me, one finish line down, a lifetime of finish lines still to come. The love of his life, Lauren, was waiting for him when he finished. And I think both of us, Jimmy and I, thanked the good lord that Lauren was there with us, to kiss Jimmy and to tell him how proud she was of him and how she loved him. I was glad that we hadn't lost Lauren on that very first night we had met her. And Jimmy was glad Lauren was there to share the rest of their lives together.

CHAPTER 7

The Truths **of Wasatch**

You don't often enter a 100-mile race with the thought that, "This race is going to teach me about what it means to be a father, and what it means to be a friend, and what my limitations are as a runner." But this is exactly what my experiences over the past five years at Utah's Wasatch Front 100 Mile Endurance Run have come to mean to me. When I first entered Wasatch in 2017, it was a hoped-for bookend to a summer of mountain racing. The plan was to finish the Bighorn 100 in Wyoming in June, then Wasatch during the first weekend after Labor Day. I didn't finish either race. A rainstorm that turned Bighorn's already challenging course into a miles-long morass of mud led to a "did not finish" (DNF) at the halfway point. My youngest daughter, Katie, also dropped out halfway while older daughter Annie gamely slipped and slid her way through the night and into the next day before missing the 3 p.m. cutoff at the Dry Fork Ridge aid station at mile 82.5. The sting of the DNF at Bighorn made Wasatch suddenly became much more important to me.

I had heard about Wasatch, which along with Western States, Old Dominion in Virginia, and Leadville in Colorado, is among the oldest trail hundred-milers in the country. Of the four, Wasatch's history might be the most unlikely, simply because the very first time it was held, it almost didn't have any finishers. It was the first of these oldest events to have a woman tie for first. Dana "Mud 'N Guts" Miller is the unquestioned historian of Wasatch, having finished the race 20 times. He's written extensively about it over the years. I interviewed Dana on the phone once while I was a sportswriter in Reno. I was working on a story about hydration packs, and not specifically about Wasatch. It was the mid-1990s when we talked. Dana had recently won Wasatch five times between 1985 and 1992, including setting the course record in 1990. He was an exuberant and highly entertaining interview. It wasn't hard to imagine him doing things like the way he celebrated his 40th birthday in September 1991 when he ran the Wasatch course *twice* for 200 miles. I asked him what made Wasatch so difficult. Dana paused for a long time. "I started running just like everybody else," Dana finally said. His deliberateness, I've come to realize years later, served almost as a warning to me to be careful and mindful of the special challenge that Wasatch presents. "I would run a few blocks, and that was all I could do. I'd cough and wheeze the rest of the day. It made me feel really tiny. Wasatch has this way of reducing you and reducing every-thing that you're doing down to its most basic. The course and what it demands of you takes on an incredible bit of significance. Just making it to the finish line at Wasatch is an incredible accomplishment. I try to never forget that."

The Roots of Wasatch

Wasatch got its start in 1980. Western States had held its first "offi-cial" race in 1977, with 14 starters and three finishers. Old Dominion, founded by Wayne and Pat Botts, who were friends of and were inspired by Tevis Cup founder Wendell Robie, followed in 1979 with 45 starters and 22 finishers. Richard Barnum-Reece, who had organized some of the very first trail ultras in Utah, came up with the idea of the Wasatch 100 during the summer of 1980. Barnum-Reece found a collaborator in ultra runner Steve Baugh, who to this day remains involved with Wasatch. Mud 'N Guts Miller has written on the Wasatch 100 website that, "Richard was loud, flamboyant, unconventional, and took pleasure in being controversial. Steve Baugh, on the other hand, was a 30-year-old Boy Scout by comparison. Steve was self-effacing, shy, and pretty well the epitome of a conservative Utahn. He was, however, tough as nails, fiercely self-reliant, and loved being in the mountains. That the inaugural Wasatch 100 blended Richard's outlandishness with Steve's quiet independence should be no surprise."

The first Wasatch 100 was held on September 27-28, 1980. It started outside of Ogden, Utah, near a place called Winder Dairy, and took runners on a point-to-point route on trails, paved and dirt roads, and sometimes passed through private property. It was to finish at Sundance Ski Resort. Almost from the very beginning, the runners were challenged well beyond the norm of any hundred-miler. The route had them go straight up a climb known as "Chinscraper." Steve Baugh, who is a highly meticulous person, did his best to create maps for the runners who did the first Wasatch. There was no registration to run Wasatch, nor were there any course markings, only Baugh's highlights traced across Forest Service quadrangle maps. Steve's wife, Evelyn, would provide aid along the way. The five entrants were Barnum-Reece, Baugh, Laurie Staton, Greg Rollins, and Jan Cheney. Staton was the only female entrant. As it turned out, the group (which more or less had agreed to run together) encountered sections where the trail disappeared. They'd bushwhack their way through thick underbrush in the general direction they knew they needed to go until they discovered more trail. At one point, they had to keep crossing and recrossing one of the area's drainages, Hardscrabble Creek. Eventually the group of five became a group of three: Staton, Baugh, and Rollins. Baugh eventually dropped out due to stomach issues. He was also worried about Barnum-Reece, who had become lost and would end up spending a cold night not far from Hardscrabble Creek before wandering back to civilization the next morning.

Staton would prove indefatigable. She had pulled ahead overnight of Rollins. By 75 miles at Brighton Ski Resort, as she was preparing to eat a breakfast of pancakes prepared by a short-order cook at the Brighton Village Store, she was surprised that she was still ahead of him. She trekked on, scaling steep Catherine Pass above Brighton before dropping into the precipitous Dry Fork drainage. In a Wasatch oral history, she said, "Somehow, I got wind that Greg Rollins was still in the race, so I decided I should stop to wait for him. After all, I thought, this trail we were traveling was an adventure, first, and a race, second. At about the top of the Alpine Loop, he finally caught up with me, and from there we ran in together." Barnum-Reece, recovered from his long, lost, sleepless night, caught up to the two runners not long after on the Alpine Loop . . . in his Volkswagen van. He began shouting out the driver's side window to "Follow me!" It was, Mud 'N Guts Miller later wrote, a typical Richard Barnum-Reece moment. He was confidently directing the two remaining runners to follow him, "possibly without a clue in the world exactly where that finish line would be . . . Somewhere near Sundance, Richard finally pulled into a gravel parking area, as Laurie and Greg arrived together, declared the very first Wasatch Front 100 Mile Endurance Run (finishers) after 35 hours, 1 minute, and 21 seconds."

Following a Treacherous Path

In 2017, I ran my first Wasatch. I had never stepped foot on the course before that September. The stories about Wasatch and its extraordinarily unique character were all out there. So many rocks that you often couldn't touch the dirt, and so much scree and cobblestones it often felt like you were trying to skate along over marbles. The long and draining start of Chinscraper replaced by the equally challenging 4.4-mile, 4,200-foot climb up Bair Canyon from the start at the East Mountain Wilderness Park in Kaysville, Utah. The nights that could often hover around freezing and leave you shivering so intensely you couldn't ever snap out of it. The infamous "Dive" and the equally infamous "Plunge," as the race worked its way past 80 miles on descents so steep you either miraculously kept moving forward or fell flat on your face. And there was the history. Not just the colorful history of Richard Barnum-Reece and Laurie Staton and the first few runners who ever attempted the race, but the historic nature of the Wasatch Front. Of all the great mountain ranges in the American West, this was the one whose near-impenetrability led to tragedy. In August 1846, the Donner Party plunged into the Wasatch as part of the largely untried "Hastings Cutoff," promoted by attorney and trail huckster Lansford Hastings in his 1845 book, *The Emigrants' Guide to Oregon and California*. The "Hastings Cutoff" promised a more direct route from the more established Oregon Trail for emigrants headed to California. As they made their way into the Wasatch, the Donner Party was met almost immediately with sheer quartz walls, followed by thickets of rock, tree, and brush that needed to be cleared by hand. It took the party nearly two weeks to get clear of the Wasatch before dropping into the Salt Lake Valley. Already well behind the schedule needed to clear the Sierra before snow made the mountains unpassable for the winter, the Donner Party's struggle through the Wasatch ensured that a winter-bound tragedy near present-day Truckee, California and Donner Lake would ensue. Of the Donner Party's 81 members, only 45 would survive. One of the survivors of the Donner Party, 13-year-old Virginia Reed, later wrote a cousin of the experience, "O Mary, I have not wrote you half the trouble we have had. Never take any cutoffs and hurry along as fast as you can."

My good trail friend Jeffrey Conner had experienced the challenge of the Wasatch 100 firsthand when he had first attempted it in 2015. It was Jeff's first hundred-miler. He admitted later that he completely underestimated what it would take to finish. The rocks, altitude, and the pounding of the relentless long ups and equally long and disruptive downs eventually did him in, and he dropped out at not long after 60 miles. In 2016, Jeff, who has been a key member of the Nevada Attorney General's office for many years, returned to Wasatch bent on redemption. If 2015 was about not fully grasping what Wasatch asks of its runners, 2016 was about knowing full well what to expect. And it was also about more than that. Jeff didn't quite realize how important his quest to finish Wasatch had become to some of his running friends. A frequent training partner, Michelle Edmonson, who at the time was a customer sales representative for Patagonia in Reno, could see how much a Wasatch finish had come to mean to Jeff.

"You don't ever think about a DNF until it happens, and then it becomes something that if you can, you want to try to … maybe 'avenge' is not the right word, but it's always something that you think about whenever it happens," Jeff says. "I just wanted to run Wasatch again with my eyes open a little bit wider."

Michelle and Jeff became friends through running trails and solidified their friendship through other commonalities like their whimsical senses of humor (Michelle often wore rainbow-colored tutus in races; Jeff had a propensity for colorful knee socks.). They also shared a love of skiing, as neither were averse to running 20 miles in our nearby Virginia City Highlands in the wintertime on a Saturday morning, then driving about 25 miles due west to Mount Rose Ski Resort to spend the rest of the day on the ski slopes. They also shared an ability to be there to help whenever others needed support or encouragement. Jeff's Wasatch in 2016 was one of those moments for Michelle, who remembered, "What's the old saying, 'Family by blood, or family by sweat?' I knew I had to be there to help my friend."

And Michelle did. She served as Jeff's only crew over the first 67 miles, driving to the early aid stations and providing him with food and positive affirmation. Then she jumped in and paced him over the final 33 miles. "Michelle carried me to the finish," Jeff said. "She was steady and strong the whole way to the end. She was funny when she could be and stern when she had to be. But most of all, she was just … there … present in the moment, selflessly adding to my incredible experience without any expectation of receiving anything in return other than getting a front row seat to watch her friend succeed and overcome adversity." For Michelle, her actions that Wasatch weekend didn't feel particularly noble or worth any extra attention. "It's what friends do for other friends," she said. One of Michelle's good friends and another key contributor to our running group, Kaycee Green, put it well: "This sport touches a unique part of the soul that seems to be awakened when you get to share it with those people whose souls speak that same language."

Wasatch battered me worse than any race I'd ever run in my life when I ran it in 2017. The day was hot, into the 80s. I foolishly ran too hard over the first 30 miles, not realizing how it would cost me later. I ran on adrenalin once the sun went down, and Katie was pacing me through what I've been told is one of the most beautiful parts of the course in the daytime, the aspen-lined five-mile section that runs from the Big Water aid station to the Desolation Lake aid station. The adrenalin pumped as we were only a couple of miles from Desolation Lake when Katie and I and another group of runners were stopped dead in our tracks by a pair of eyes that glowed an exotic silver white in the night at a height that looked like they belonged on a tall stepladder rather than a particular kind of animal. I had seen moose before, when I had run in the Bighorns of Wyoming, but at a far-off distance. This moose was only a few yards away and wasn't moving. When it finally stepped off the trail, it did so loudly, with the heavy brush collapsing underneath it like an empty cardboard box. We waited a few minutes as it still lingered close by. Then we made a break for it. We sprinted by it, and then like Indiana Jones being chased by the massive boulder in *Indiana Jones and the Temple of Doom*, our heads down, allowing ourselves only somewhat muffled squeals and not the screams we had felt building up inside of us, we ran at top speed for several hundred yards before we turned to see if the moose had given chase. It hadn't. We stopped and high-fived and cheered. "We made it!" one of the runners we'd joined exclaimed. "We're still alive!"

That would be the most alive I would feel. My race began deteriorating not long after. I got a fresh pacer, Jeffrey, at the Brighton Sky Resort at mile 68. After we had made the 2.7-mile, climb out of Brighton to the top of Catherine Pass, I began leaning, more than likely from overexerting earlier in the day when it was so hot out. My lean wasn't bad at first. Every so often, as we made the two-mile descent to the Ant Knolls aid station, Jeffrey would give me a gentle reminder. "Try to lean a little more the other way, buddy," he'd say. I would self-consciously then straighten up a bit, like I was sitting in a classroom and had just been asked a question by a teacher I wished to please. I would lean as hard as I could to my left. I couldn't maintain it, though, and found myself gripping my trekking poles even tighter in an attempt to keep myself straight. I suddenly felt like I could understand how it felt to be dependent on a walking stick or a walker as you grew older. Hundred-milers are supposed to be an affirmation of our steely determination to push through the difficulties and demonstrate how strong we are. Instead, I was growing weaker, my lean becoming more pronounced by the moment. I was hoping when the sun came up again, the prospect of a new day might rally me and make my body magically straighten again. The opposite happened. As we moved from sunrise to mid-morning, I was having difficulty keeping my balance. I'd trip and fall. The "Dive" and the "Plunge" outside of the mile 85-mile Pot Hollow aid station were exercises in excruciating pain and a flood of frustration. Both the "Dive" and the "Plunge" were like running down the eroded sides of a skyscraper. They were extreme drops that in my diminished state felt like I was falling down a chute littered with so many rocks and trail that was so steeply rutted there was no possible way for me to stay upright. I fell and cursed and fell again. I was wearing Wasatch now, the gray dust of the trail like an exploding gray cloud all over my shorts and running shirt.

As we made our way through the tall, cool grass that led to mile 85, we were met by the Pot Hollow aid station captain, Mark Robbins. Mark, his family, and all of the other aid station volunteers were a welcoming presence. The entire aid station spoke to efficiency and experience. Mark's wife, Sarah, brought me food and an ice-cold Sprite to drink. The aid station volunteers, with less than an hour to go before the aid station's cutoff would hit, were busily doing the things an aid station that knows what it is doing does. There was an assembly line of Zip-Loc bags being filled with watermelon and chips, so that as the final runners would come through Pot Hollow, they could quickly be given the bags to carry with them so as not to waste any time standing and waiting for help from the volunteers. The Robbins' kids—daughter Riley, 18, and sons Camden, 16, and Cooper, 15—were right in the middle of the Zip-Loc assembly line. I had told Jeff earlier that my lean had become too much of a danger to me. I couldn't see all of the trail I was running on, and my back and hips were throbbing. Mark, with raven hair and a salt-and-pepper beard, was at 5-foot-9 and 210 pounds a stoutly built former wrestler. He looked tough. But his voice was surprisingly soft and tender. He asked me, as I sipped at the Sprite Sarah had handed me, if I was sure I wanted to drop out. I told him yes, and then I started to cry. Mark wrapped me in his arms and told me, "Everything is going to be OK. You'll be back again. That's why it's Wasatch. You're never through with Wasatch until Wasatch tells you it's through with you." Mark seemed to be the perfect person for an aid station like Pot Hollow, where dreams can either be dashed or you can dash off with less than an hour left before the cutoff in an attempt to still realize them. Just a few minutes after he'd comforted me, I saw him startle another runner who was complaining he didn't have enough time to still make the finish.

"Not with that attitude you won't," Mark said. His words were like cold water splashed on the runner's face. The runner stopped his complaining and snapped to it. He grabbed his bag from one of the Robbins kids, high-fived Mark his thanks, and then marched off from the aid station, still in the running to make it to the finish line.

Sometimes an End Is Really a Beginning

I've often wondered why that DNF wasn't an ending with Wasatch. Perhaps the disappointment of not finishing and wanting to redeem myself by running it again was part of it. But that only speaks to part of why Wasatch has been so important to me. My lean led to a DNF, but it also opened my eyes. If everything had gone smoothly, Jeffrey and I would've popped up into Pot Hollow through the promise of better times just ahead, through that tall grass and the majestic aspens that lead you into Pot Hollow and then on to the finish. If I hadn't dropped out, we wouldn't have stopped and spent time with Mark Robbins. We would've grabbed some fluids and some food and stayed in the tunnel vision that tells you there are less than 15 miles to go and that's what you need to do . . . you need to go. You don't stop. The last stages of hundred-milers and the last few aid stations become like drive-throughs, where voices and faces can become disconnected and diffuse. My DNF slowed everything down. The drive-through feeling was replaced by human connection and empathy. If I hadn't DNF'd, I wouldn't have come to learn Mark's story and how it would help me understand the experiences my own two daughters would have running Wasatch. Sometimes when we fail, there is an inevitability that it will narrow our focus even more, and make us become so obsessed with the thing that made us fail that we lose all sense of what is happening on the periphery of our lives. In my case, not finishing Wasatch made what was happening on the periphery become the focus of how I viewed this incredibly grueling race. It reminded me, as Mud 'N Guts Miller had mentioned in that phone conversation from long ago, how small I was and how large the lives and accomplishments of others were to become to me. In this sense, failure at Wasatch became one of my most important victories.

Mark Robbins' life was a great example. Mark and I stayed connected after my DNF, and we became friends. What I found so intriguing about Mark was how his story of becoming an ultra runner was so unlikely. He was 41 when I met him in 2017, married to Sarah for 20 years. He had grown up in an athletic Utah family, one of five brothers and two sisters. Along with his brothers, Mark had been a champion high school wrestler (and several of his brothers went on to wrestle collegiately as well). His life in Cottonwood Heights, Utah, was a busy one. He was director of surgery for a healthcare staffing company. He and Sarah never missed any of their kids' many school activities. Yet there was also a growing sense of sadness. During a two-year span, he lost six members of his family (grandparents, nieces, and nephews) as well as a couple of friends. He was regularly attending memorial services and feeling not only his own sense of loss, but the anguish of those who were directly experiencing it. "You can only absorb so much of that kind of sadness before it really gets to you," he said. "I was a pallbearer too many times over too short a period." So he turned to an unlikely activity, running, which during his wrestling days had only been used as a means to cut weight for a match or as a way to toughen or punish himself. This time he used it as therapy. He began training for local road races. "It was fun," he said, "but I don't know if it fulfilled me completely in the way that it should have."

Mark was also a lifelong hunter. It just so happened that not long after he'd begun running, he spent a September night during hunting season in Parley's Canyon, located on the western slope of the Wasatch, just outside of Salt Lake City. Parley's has always been a place of transition and new paths, having served even as early as the 1840s as part of the Pony Express overland mail route. It was the evening of the first Friday after Labor Day when Mark saw some far-off lights. The lights moved with a deliberate steadiness, slowly snaking their way up the spine of the canyon. Mark turned to one of his hunting friends.

"What is that?" he asked.

"That's the Wasatch 100," his friend replied. "And those are the headlamps of the runners. They're running 100 miles."

Mark felt something stir inside of him. When he had wrestled, there was always the rush of competition that had excited him, the feeling of knowing soon his body would be filled with a torrent of adrenalin and the impending crashes of physical contact with another wrestler. This was different. It felt as if a voice in the night was calling him to join the Wasatch runners. That in their presence he might find something meaningful, something that might tell him about who he was and what he still might become. "I get goosebumps every time I think about that moment, that moment when I saw those headlamps of the Wasatch runners," Mark said. "It hit me really hard. I knew right then. I knew right at that moment as I am sitting there in the dark that I wanted to run that race."

Mark volunteered for Wasatch in 2011. He ran it and finished it, in 34:36, in 2012.

"When people ask, 'Why would you ever do that race?' I half in jest tell them, 'Well, because I was called to it,'" he said. "In a lot of ways, though, that's the truth. It appeared to me at the side of the road that night. And from that moment on, it's helped me. Becoming an ultra runner changed everything. It's helped me gain clarity. It lifted me from the abyss."

When I met Mark while serving as the aid station captain of Pot Hollow in 2017, I shouldn't have been surprised that he was volunteering and giving back.

"The sport has basically given me my life back," he said. "Because of that, I always felt that I have to give back. Helping others accomplish their goals is worth more than any finisher's buckle I'm ever going to earn. Helping others do extraordinary things is one of the most rewarding things I've ever done in my life."

See You at the Finish: Passing Down Lessons from the Trail

Knowing Mark and his story has also provided me fresh perspective on what it means to be a father, particularly a running father of children who are also runners. Recently Mark told me the story of his son Cooper's first 50K. Cooper has always been the Robbins family member who has taken the most time in figuring out his path. "Coop's plans often are which way the wind blows," Mark said, with a gentle laugh. Cooper is an exceptionally bright young man, and like his father, he was a wrestler along with playing football and running cross country and track in high school. In August 2021, after graduating a couple of months earlier from Skyline High School in Salt Lake City, Cooper ran the El Vaquero Loco 50K in Wyoming's Bridger-Teton National Forest. Mark was running an accompanying 25K race that day, and saw Cooper, who had made the turnaround for the 50K and was headed back to the finish. The son gave the father a quick wave and a smile. Later, when Cooper wrote an essay about his experience for a class he was taking at Salt Lake City Community College, he wrote about how all of his past experiences had helped pull him through to the finish (which he reached in a touch over nine hours), noting that, "I had already powered through many setbacks leading up to this race, so I felt unstoppable. . . . I remember the joy I felt when I realized that I was going to finish this race and make my younger self proud as well as make my current self proud." Mark remembered reading Cooper's essay and thinking that his son had achieved a sense of self-awareness that Mark at a similar age wasn't even close to attaining. There was a sense, Mark said, that his 18-year-old son was now starting to exceed some of Mark's accomplishments and understanding what those accomplishments might mean as his life progressed. "It was really touching to me," Mark said, "to know that Cooper was already understanding how time on the trail helps ground you and helps make you a better person . . . how when things go wrong you keep working and make the necessary adjustments . . . how when you get to a hill that seems insurmountable, you still find your way up that hill. To know that he had already figured these things out was really, totally humbling to me as a father."

I've had a remarkably similar and humbling experience in watching my two daughters run and finish Wasatch. Annie finished Wasatch in 2018 in 35:33. Katie finished Wasatch twice, in 33:52 in 2019 and then, on the final leg of her successful quest to achieve the Grand Slam of ultra running—or completion of four of the nation's four oldest hundred-milers in one summer—she finished in 34:49 in 2021. In all three races, my daughters ran with a supreme sense of confidence. Wasatch wore them down, but it never stopped either of them.

Annie prepared for Wasatch throughout the summer of 2018 on some of the toughest terrain we have in our area. She had finished Western States in 2016 and knew that Wasatch was going to provide a different sort of challenge. She sought out high-elevation runs, above 8,000 feet, and trained herself to eat and drink huge amounts of food and fluid while she was running. Annie, who is now married and a mother to twins, has been around the sport from her earliest days. When I ran my first ultra in 1995, she was six years old. She can still remember sleeping in a tent at trackside of the Placer High School finish line at Western States, and then gradually becoming aware that she wanted to one day be a finisher who ran on that same track. She wrote in a college essay one time that to her, finishing these long races was a personal achievement but also an experience where "you share so much with everyone: the people you admire and love, the crews, the pacers, the volunteers, the fellow runners with whom you share the trail . . . When you finish, you finish for all of these people." As we stood in the darkness of East Mountain Wilderness Park on September 2018, a few moments before Annie's Wasatch was to begin, I began to realize that hers was a much wider circle of running experience than mine had ever been. Mark Robbins walked out of the darkness like he knew all along he was going to see us. He was there to see his younger brother, Brian, off on his own Wasatch journey that day. I remembered how Mark had wrapped me in a reassuring hug at Pot Hollow the year before when I dropped out. Before Annie had even started, Mark wrapped her in a hug and told her she was on her way to having an amazing day. "I'll see you at the finish," he confidently told Annie. Over the next 35 hours, Annie moved steadily forward, with the wisdom of a veteran runner, a runner whose whole physical aspect contains not only the color of movement of today, but of tomorrow. It was still early September, and she was still in her 20s. It was hard not to imagine, however, as she kept moving and never faltered. The day heated, and the pinwheel pink flamingoes that greet the runners at the Big Mountain aid station at mile 30 remained so perfectly still you wondered if you might see them starting to melt, perhaps taking Annie's race along with them. Annie trotted right past them and didn't give the day's heat a second thought. In the middle of the night when she came into Brighton Ski Resort and fell asleep for a few moments still clutching a cup of warm chicken broth, I could sense that there was a silent synchronization going on inside of her. That when it soon turned to autumn, she would be ready for the change in seasons, that by pressing relentlessly on at Wasatch, by always moving forward, she had been growing, learning the value of pressing on. I remember the joy we felt when she crossed the finish line on Saturday afternoon at Soldier Hollow, paced by Katie for nearly 47 miles and then over the final nearly 10 miles by her boyfriend (and now husband and father to twins Owen and Isabelle), Steve. The real-time celebration melted for me into something more: memories of Annie as a little girl running with me on the track at the finish of Western States, her hand so small it felt like it belonged to a little doll, Annie running with a barefoot Katie on the track at the finish of her own Western States, Annie coming up the long black road of asphalt leading to the Soldier Hollow finish line grass whose green had almost turned a bleached yellow from the quickly waning heat of summer. Jill and I both cried our eyes out as we saw Annie cross the finish line, greeted by the welcoming, grandfatherly presence of Wasatch's longtime race director, John Grobben. As much as that moment was about her triumph of finishing, I also couldn't help but feel the presence of the future. She'd already exceeded my Pot Hollow DNF a year earlier by pushing on through for an additional 15 miles. She'd succeeded where I had failed. Surrounded by friends, family, and well-wishers at the Wasatch finish, she was where I had always hoped I'd be. My Mark Robbins hug had been one of sympathetic reassurance. Annie's Mark Robbins hug had been one of confident expectation. See you at the finish. Her maturity as a seasoned ultra runner hadn't allowed Wasatch to break her. She had grown in an immeasurable way and seemed capable of handling anything she would ever encounter in her life.

Success is a Community Effort

Of Katie's two Wasatch finishes, the one that best encapsulated her was in 2019. What made it special was how it was a shared effort involving one of the best people we've ever known. We had first met Juan more than a decade earlier. He had arrived in the United States as a teenager, having come across the border from Mexico to escape violence, but was detained and sent back to Mexico. Juan tried again three days later and made a successful crossing into the United States, and was soon running and working as a machinist in Reno. There is a quiet nobility to everything that Juan does, from being the friend who drops everything he is doing to supporting your latest crazy running endeavor to helping his wife, Lacey, foster large numbers of dogs and cats at their home. He can have the patience and the humility to sit for hours at a time at a sewing machine to create his own running shorts and shirts or to sit at an adjoining table while taking a file and some scissors and molding a pair of running shoes into a mild artform that fits his feet with a jeweler's precision. Juan is also a runner whose endurance seems never ending. He has done things that make even the most seasoned ultra runner blink in amazement. In 2014, he ran the entire 178-mile Reno Tahoe Odyssey, which is usually done in relay fashion by teams of up to 12 runners into the mountains above Reno and then on the paved roads around all of Lake Tahoe before descending back down from the historic silver rush town of Virginia City into Reno, solo. Juan's friends donned T-shirts that had his face on them, with the words "An Army of Juan" proudly proclaiming their allegiance to that weekend's cause. Juan finished in 46 hours and 20 minutes. There may not be a more respected nor beloved trail runner in all of northern Nevada than Juan. He and Lacey (who, by the way, was with Lauren Watson that fateful first run where we almost lost Lauren) were married on June 29, 2018 in a verdant valley on a beautiful early evening with wisps of clouds coloring a blue sky not far from the oldest town in Nevada, Genoa. It was perhaps the biggest social event the trail community of northern Nevada had ever seen. Lacey was lovely in a white dress, her shoulders bare and flowers in her brown hair. Juan was handsome in a black suit, purple vest, and purple tie. We danced the night away in celebration of two beloved people, one born in Mexico and the other born in Illinois. Juan danced that night the same way he moves on the trails: flawlessly. His stride has always been short, efficient, and so light his knees hardly lift. He's told me many times that it's the joy of being in nature, and particularly in the mountains, where he feels most at home. You can sense this joy whenever you are with him, that he is being shaped by the bigness of the places where we run, where the trails can be narrow but the vistas expansive beyond all imagination. Juan has always been an undaunted explorer, his many travels and adventures an index to his character that seeks out the toughest climbs and the most challenging running routes.

So it wasn't that surprising when we learned that Juan had been battling a series of injuries throughout the summer of 2019, and with only a single 20-mile run under his belt in preparation, that he was still determined to run Wasatch that September. But as is often the case in ultra running, Juan wouldn't be alone as he attempted the distance so sorely short of training. As it turned out, Juan would have company that would help pull him through the entire distance. Katie and Juan, who had been friends since Katie had been a young runner in high school, ran pretty much the entire Wasatch together. Katie's philosophy of running has always centered on two things: Run your best, and make friends along the way. "If you don't make any friends, then what's the point?" she has said more than once over the years. Her Wasatch run in 2019 was all about friendship. She and Juan crossed underneath Wasatch's red-lettered finish line banner together and turned immediately toward one another. They had strengthened each other's weak spots, making the mindless labor of running 100 miles meaningful. Katie's sunny nature and positive assurances kept Juan's sparse preparation stoked enough to go the distance. Juan's low-kneed running so soundless of foot and breath was a 100-mile-long reminder to Katie that the longest distances only surrender their challenge when you run as Juan has always run, when you are at peace with yourself. Yet again, my child had exceeded me by a wide margin with her experience at Wasatch. Katie had enough inner strength to enable not only herself, but her good friend, to get to the finish line as well. Their race together cemented my faith in human nature.

Connection Is the Top Prize

I don't know if I truly understood what running was about until I attempted to run Wasatch, and then watched some of the people I know and love run Wasatch. As runners, we start out chasing the things we wish to conquer—time and distance. We wish to run as fast as we can, for as long as we can. Even if we slow, and time becomes less of a motivator, covering the sheer ultra marathon distances remain our primary intoxicant. As I've grown older, and as my body has told me in no uncertain terms that it is acutely aware of what I am trying to do to it, the allure has been less about time and distance and more about every human's wish to remain connected with other people. This has become more of an imperative as I've run into my 50s. I had no earthly idea when I was a young runner that I would need this essential connection so much as I grew to be an older runner. I remember reading the words of one of my favorite writers, the legendary *New Yorker* writer and editor Roger Angell, who at age 93 wrote an amazing book, *This Old Man*, which took an unsparing, sometimes funny, but often deeply moving look at growing old. He wrote of our basic need as we get older to know that as we live, we always crave companionship to make it come to life: "Getting old is the second-biggest surprise of my life, but the first, by a mile, is our unceasing need for deep attachment and intimate love."

My experiences with Wasatch brought this into full focus for me. The course was incredibly difficult and without question one of the ultimate challenges in ultra running. Everywhere you turn at Wasatch there is difficulty. The rocks are sharper and more plentiful than at other races. The climbs are so dusty, steep, and exhausting you can't help but close your eyes and, as the sweat stings your eyeballs from the effort, feel as if you have become an honorary member of the ill-fated Donner Party, forever lost in a maze of misery and uncertainty. Somehow Wasatch in September had become the place where I could feel the pangs of my own running mortality. It had bent my back in such a way that I was leaning and falling over in 2017, ultimately bringing me to tears in Mark Robbins' arms when I dropped out at Pot Hollow aid station. If I had let it, Wasatch could have remained a frightening apparition to me for the rest of my days, making the rightness of all that I'd ever done in running feel like it had all been time that had been wasted. I didn't want Wasatch to become such a strict pronouncement. Instead, the hard realities of Wasatch made me seek out the comfort of family, friendships, and relationships. These are the pillows we rest our heads upon whenever we grow uncertain, or anxious, or even scared, about growing older each year. It gave me some comfort. More than that, it made me grow.

Earlier this year I had a phone conversation with Nick Bassett. In September 2021, Nick, who is retired and who lives most of the year in Wyoming and the other part of the year wherever his longtime partner, Barbara Elias, an ultra runner and traveling orthopedic physician's assistant, happens to be working, became at age 76 the oldest runner to ever finish Wasatch—twice. The front end of his "double" began three years earlier in 2018, when Nick, at age 73, became the oldest finisher at Western States. To the best of my knowledge, he's the first person to ever be the oldest finisher at two of the oldest hundred-mile races in the world. Having only covered 85 miles of the Wasatch course myself, I had to ask Nick, who is almost old enough to be my father, what his secret of going the entire distance was in September 2022. "I got lonely," Nick said. "I didn't want to have go so much of the distance alone." So about halfway through the race, at the Lambs Canyon aid station near an Interstate 80 underpass leading back into the mountains, Nick reached out to another runner, 59-year-old Colleen Ford, a longtime and very accomplished runner from Utah. Nick asked if he could run with Colleen and her pacer, a friend named Karen Helfrich. "Of course," Colleen told Nick. "You're welcome to tag along." Nick knew that as long as he had company and stayed with the women who would quickly become his friends over the next 52 miles, "I was going to make it. I knew as long as we kept each other company, we were all going to make it to the finish." Nick finished three hundred-milers during the summer of his 76th year. His secret? Great genes? Great training? Great determination? Well, maybe. More importantly, "I just try to find somebody at the races I run these days. We help each other, and we keep each other company, and we make it to the finish together." As I heard a now 77-year-old man's voice on the phone, it was hard not to also hear my 29-year-old daughter's as well. Nick was the same kind of runner as Katie. They ran races to test themselves. But they also ran races communally, as a way to share the experience and to make friends. The bond connecting our age with our youth could not have been more apparent, or stronger, as I thought about how Nick and Katie were kind and kindred spirits.

We never lose this longing, Roger Angell has told us, to have human companionship wherever we are, whether it is in the grocery store, or at an aid station halfway through one of the world's most challenging hundred-milers. This is the truth of Wasatch. It's not necessarily the call of the mountains that we seek. If not for the people who accompany us through those mountains, the journey wouldn't be nearly as relatable, nor as worthy. We need stories—not just our own stories, but stories that the people we meet share with us over the long hours of struggle and progress we make toward our next finish line. I don't know if I knew this when I began running ultras nearly 30 years ago. Now, thanks to the experiences I've had and the experiences I've witnessed at Wasatch, I do.

PART **THREE**

Overcoming Your
Challenges

CHAPTER 8

Remembering the Runner You Were, **and Knowing the Runner You Are**

Memory can be an elusive thing. To gather its many elements into a coherent, meaningful narrative can be pretty futile, like trying to grab leaves blown crazily down a sidewalk by a roaring leaf blower. Increasingly, as I've grown older, my memories of my running long ago have become like this. If I do remember much of the runner I was, it has come to inhabit a place where the shadows are cool and solitary, mixed with a vague sense of pride and melancholy. Since my microfracture knee surgery in 2007, I've searched for the runner I once was, while evolving into the runner I am now. Make no mistake, though: I like the runner I am now. The runner I am now is more helpful, more concerned for others and less worried about himself. The runner I am now takes time to hug and to listen. The runner I am now tries to contribute to our community. The runner I am now, I think, has taken memory and made it plural, collecting and sharing it with others. There is a part of me that is perfectly content with the fact that I may or may not be able to run like I once did pre-surgery. If anything, the years that have passed since 2007 have taught me that the simple act of running is a miraculous thing, a gift really, and to take it for granted or cloud it with too-harsh judgments or negative thoughts based on placing or finish time is simply a fool's errand.

Life—and the Trail—Can Throw an Unexpected Curveball

I can still remember the sound of the articular cartilage in my right knee shredding on that May day in the Marin Headlands in 2007. I was above a spot known as Pirate's Cove, on a picture-postcard trail that snaked along coastal cliffs that looked down upon the crashing waves of the Pacific Ocean. I was about 15 or 16 miles into that year's Miwok 100K, moving with the restrained joy that comes with knowing you are in the best shape of your life. My plan was to unleash my high-fitness level on the second half of the course and run with abandon to the finish line. I was building up to what I expected to be my greatest finish at Western States ever. The entire winter and spring had been one personal best effort after another. Our group runs on Tuesday and Thursday nights after work were such that I could arrive a good 10 or 15 minutes behind everyone and still catch everyone before the end. One night I surged past one of my friends, Lon Monroe, so quickly and locomotive-like that he feigned like I had created a cold, hard wind that had just whipped against him. "Mr. Trent! You're running faster than anyone should on a Tuesday night!" Lon called out to me. "I can't help myself," I called back, gleefully, over my shoulder. "This all feels too good not to keep going!"

And then on the trail above Pirates Cove, transfixed for only perhaps a second or two by the Pacific's foamy beauty beneath the trail, I didn't pay close enough attention to the trail. My right foot jammed momentarily against a rock. Nothing was out of the ordinary about it. No shooting pain. No dramatic limp. Just a light cracking sound, like someone noisily eating a bowl of cereal. About 50 yards later, my knee stiffened. Still nothing too alarming. I slowed to a walk, shook my leg once or twice, and the stiffness seemed to subside. I started running again. Everything felt fine for the next 20 miles or so. I kept to my plan and started to pick up the pace over the back half of the race, as Miwok transitioned from the coast to inland, into Muir Woods, into old-growth Redwoods and bright green ferns peeking pleasantly out from beneath the thick canopy. I swooped down each downhill like a runner possessed. It was the uphills that began to tell me that something was awry. I am normally a strong climber and love to run uphill. For whatever reason, any climb would force my knee to stiffen. If I tried to run, the knee would stiffen as it had near Pirates Cove. The more I tried to run any uphill, the more my knee would object, tightening so much I was better off walking. I adjusted immediately. I ran like a madman on any downhill (I didn't feel any pain on any downhill). Then I would shift to a vigorous hike whenever there was a climb. I finished the race with my fastest time ever at Miwok, pleased that I hadn't let that uphill stiffness of my knee derail my race. Western States was only about seven weeks away at that point. "Another building block in place," I remember telling Lon after he had made his way to the finish at a windy Rodeo Beach.

I never made it to Western States that year. The next day I could barely bend my knee. There was swelling around the outside of my knee, or what I came to learn was the "lateral aspect" of my articular cartilage. In subsequent x-rays and an MRI, I learned all about what articular cartilage is. Articular cartilage is a very specialized connective tissue that helps provide a smooth, lubricated surface for the kneecap to move. There aren't a lot of blood vessels in articular cartilage for healing, so when you shred the articular cartilage in your medial and lateral condyle, as I did when I kicked that rock above Pirates Cove, the orthopedic surgery options available usually center around a procedure known as a "microfracture." Microfractures were becoming more common in 2007. My doctor, Dr. Ryan Dobbs, first cleaned out the damaged cartilage in an arthroscopy and then created a series of small holes in the bone. The "microfracture" penetrated the bone in such a way to allow a deeper, more rich blood supply to access the surface of my knee joint. The blood cells, he explained after I'd come out surgery that July, had a good chance of getting to the surface of the cartilage, stimulating what he called "a kind of new cartilage, a kind of baby cartilage," that would form in and around the damaged cartilage area.

Jill was with me when Dr. Dobbs, a kind, youthful-looking doctor who had a great bedside manner in that he always listened carefully to everything I had to say before honestly and thoughtfully answering every question I asked, explained how the procedure had gone that day.

"So I'll be able to run again?" I asked.

Dr. Dobbs paused. He was still in his scrubs, and his powder blue surgeon's cap was pressed backward on his head, the way a cowboy might tilt his hat back after a long day on the range. I remember thinking that he looked like a person who had already put in a full day's work, though I had been first in line and was his first knee procedure of that morning.

"Well, microfractures require a lot of patience," Dr. Dobbs said carefully. "It's going to take some time to heal. And then you're going to have to baby it so you can have the best chance for it to take. I don't know about running . . . "

Jill cut Dr. Dobbs off in mid-sentence. Her words were so abrupt and so definitive they caught both of us, Dr. Dobbs and me, off-guard.

"Not running again isn't an option for John. I hope you know that, Dr. Dobbs," Jill said.

I remember she took my hand in hers.

Dr. Dobbs smiled. We had had many discussions at prior appointments about how important running was to me.

"Well," he said, sounding like he was negotiating his way out of a hostage situation, "I know you're going to be the best patient you can possibly be. I've come to know that about you already, John. Your post-op stuff isn't going to be a problem, though you are going to have to be incredibly patient and realize this isn't going to be a linear process. So . . . if you do everything that is asked of you, yeah, maybe running half-marathons again or something like that wouldn't be out of the question."

Jill looked at me with a mixture of relief and anxiety. Relief in knowing that indeed, not running again wasn't an option. Anxiety in knowing that the days, weeks, months, and even years ahead weren't going to be easy. Dr. Dobbs was right about that part. There would be incredible highs and lows I would experience on my way back to running. But I always knew, based on how viscerally my wife had reacted when one of the nicest and most empathetic orthopedic surgeons you would ever encounter had suggested that I not run again, that even as I faced more than a few disappointing and depressing days, I wasn't going to be alone as I began my journey to become a runner again.

Get Over Yourself and Keep Running

We would meet, Lon and I, almost like we were consummating a nighttime drug deal. We'd park at one of the more popular running spots in Reno, Virginia Lake, a mile-long loop of water constructed in Reno during the 1930s by young New Deal WPA workers. Lon would sit for a few minutes in his gray Ford Expedition with the license plate "SUB 24" honoring his sub-24-hour finish at age 56 at Western States in 2003. I would wait in my green Saturn wagon until I would see Lon, who was changing out of his work clothes into his running clothes, exit his car. Then I would join him. This was the winter of 2007-2008. Lon, too, had gone through knee surgery that summer after an accumulation of wear and tear—an original high school football injury and surgery from when he was growing up in northern California in the mid-1960s had been exacerbated by years of hard living followed by years of hard running. Lon was a successful businessperson in the food supply industry, a father, a husband, a gruff-talking friend who always told you hard truths you might not want to always hear, and a recovering addict for more than two decades at that point. I had met him a decade before as our paths training for Western States had crossed. I was immediately drawn to Lon's ability to be an incredibly kind and supportive person and without question one of the hardest-edged people I'd ever encountered. He was about 15 years older than I was, and his life experience far eclipsed mine. He'd made money, and he'd lost money. He'd been a great father and an absent father. He'd burned bridges and made amends. He had stories where he was perilously on the edge of financial and personal ruin, his business dealings and his relationships in tatters, that always pointed to how lucky he had been to finally get clean and attend AA meetings. Lon's commitment to his sobriety was such that each week, even though his days of addiction and wild behavior were long behind him, he would make the 45-minute drive without fail from Reno to Incline Village, a small ski town on the waters of Lake Tahoe, to attend the same AA meeting he had always attended over the previous two decades. This type of single-minded commitment was evident in Lon's approach to ultra running. He never missed a long run with our group as we prepared for our upcoming summer hundred miles. Bad weather was never a deterrent. In fact, it was often an accelerant.

Once, a new runner to our group asked why we were running on an incredibly sloppy and muddy Peavine Mountain. The wind howled about us with such force it practically took us off our feet. We had just managed to climb up a hill that was an escalator of slippery mud that had forced us to take two steps forward, then slide a step back. It would've been grist for a comedy if not for how frustrating it had felt.

"Why are we even out doing this today?" the new runner asked Lon. "Why didn't we just sleep in today and come out later, when the weather was going to be nicer?"

"Let me ask you a question," Lon replied immediately. "When you're 75 miles into your hundred-miler this summer, and you've run through mud or water and your shoes are soaked or there's been brutal heat and you've been sweating like a malaria victim for hours or you've been pounded by winds every step of the way and you feel like you can't stand up anymore, what are you going to do? Are you just going to say, 'I've come far enough. This is good enough for today. I think 75 miles is enough'?"

"What we're experiencing right now is for that final 25 miles when you tell yourself you have no choice but to keep moving on. If you don't come out here and experience all that we're experiencing right now, on a really tough day, what are you going to do when things get really tough in a hundred-miler? I can tell you right now that what we're experiencing is a drop in a bucket compared to how tough things are going to seem when you run one hundred miles."

Then Lon shot a frown at the new runner.

"Any other thoughts?"

The new runner shook his head no.

"Then get over yourself," Lon barked. "Quit feeling sorry for yourself. And let's keep running."

Lon was tough love personified. But he was also big-hearted. I leaned on both sides of him in the months after my microfracture. At Virginia Lake, in the winter evenings of December through February of 2007-2008, we ran our first post-surgery miles together. I had been on crutches for almost eight weeks after my microfracture, then had undergone a rigorous physical therapy regimen in the fall and into the early winter. As I met Lon for our evening runs at Virginia Lake, first a few tentative jogs of a few hundred yards, then a quarter of a mile, then a half mile, then one continuous mile, I kept his words of advice about things always being tougher than we anticipate in mind. It was having the will to prepare that mattered. As long as I wanted to keep showing up at Virginia Lake, Lon did, too. I could tell that he was in even greater pain than I was. I ran with a bit of a hitch in my gait; each time before my right foot would make contact with the ground, I could feel my heel instinctively pull up and back, like it was trying to avoid making full contact with the road, reacting as if the asphalt were made of hot coals. Lon ran with a flat-out limp. His head bobbed from side to side, and he ran bull-legged. All of his effort was seemingly focused on making sure he was pointing his head, waist, and legs to the side, his body maybe hesitant of the possible pain that would shoot through it if he were to nail a straight and true footfall. It became obvious after a few weeks that I was making more progress than Lon was, though we never mentioned it to each other. He had given his word that he would be there for me as I made my recovery from my microfracture—and he was. His knee was still a problem, and even his surgeon had told him after his knee surgery, "This may or may not fix the problem. You're basically bone on bone at this point." To which Lon replied, and mentioned often to us all afterward, in words that were pure Lon: "Aren't we all, in one way or another, bone on bone?" A few years later, our friend Scott Glogovac, a Reno attorney with a fondness for really bad cinema, was preparing for his first Leadville hundred-miler. To prepare for Leadville's near-constant 10,000-foot altitude, Scott spent a lot of his summer training on the Tahoe Rim Trail. Scott had a couple of long runs where he couldn't find many takers, as the TRT, though beautiful, could be hot and exhausting with its high altitude that often took runners over passes that reached 9,000 or 10,000 feet. Scott did find a taker in Lon, though, who met his friend on several Saturday mornings on the TRT, his knee still bothersome, his limp still noticeable. Lon would grit out 20 miles or more with Scott, not because Lon was hoping to train for anything in the future, but because this was what friendship meant to him. Like so many of the people I've come to know through ultra running over the years, Lon was always the best kind of friend. He could tell stories full of the irony and absurdity of life, like the time he was running in a 50-mile race in the early 2000s. Lon happened to be running with three other runners from Northern California, all of whom were about the same age as he was. One was a judge. Another was a defense attorney. A third was a prosecutor. "And there I was," Lon laughed. "That's what makes our sport so great. You can have a guy who used to be on drugs running with a guy who probably could've defended me, next to the guy who was trying to throw me in jail, next to the guy who was going to decide if I deserved to be in jail or stay out on the streets. And do you know what? We're all great friends. Only in ultra running can this happen."

Listen to Yourself . . . and Your Body

Over time, I learned that I would need to make some concessions to my running. In the years that followed—it took me until 2009 to run my first ultra, and it wasn't until 2011 that I finished a hundred-miler—my knee couldn't withstand the rigors of daily running. Sometime in 2009, I began to run only on Tuesdays, Thursdays, and Saturdays. My knee reacted favorably, and I've been following that same regimen ever since. I also found that the running lives of the people I love—Jill, Annie, and Katie—began to become increasingly important to me. Katie and Jill both finished their first hundred-milers in 2015 (at Western States and Zion, respectively), and Annie finished her first hundred-miler in 2016 (at Western States). I crewed, paced, and supported them on all of these runs.

Jill's Zion finish was especially poignant to me. My wife has never been the fastest of runners, nor has she ever aspired to be that way. She turned to trail running in the early 2000s as a young mother who like all young mothers needed time away from work, from home, from family. She would take our dogs, first faithful little Jessie, who was a mix of a lot of small dogs, then constant companion half-rottweiler, half-lab Woody, then hall of fame-caliber black lab Penney, and white and black princess of perfection pit bull mix Willow, with her on many of her runs. There were never any record-breaking runs, but you could always count on Jill to get them all done, and to rarely, if ever, complain about the conditions. Because this is who my wife is. She isn't a complainer, and she always completes everything she starts. When she told poor Dr. Dobbs that not running was not an option for me following my microfracture surgery, she meant it. She knew how important running was to me. She never let me miss a physical therapy appointment, and whenever I was down because, as Dr. Dobbs had predicted, the recovery and return to running was never clean and linear, she was always there to cheer me up and remind me that I had vowed I was going to be the "best patient" the doctors and the physical therapists had ever seen in their lives. If there was a guiding force in my return to running, it had been Jill. She has always known me better than anyone. And she has always encouraged me, in countless aid stations, in countless ultras, and throughout our life together, to never stop moving forward.

This was why her Zion 100 finish was so special. The day in April 2015 had been hot and the course, with its many miles of running over slickrock the color of the Martian surface proved to be much more challenging that anyone from our Reno contingent could have imagined. Jill discovered that there is nothing slick about slickrock, which in theory is defined as smooth, weathered sandstone. When wet, it can become dangerously slick, as the cowboys of southern Utah in the 19th century could attest, as their horse's hoofs, especially when moving at high speeds, would slip out from underneath them because the rock had gotten so slick, hence the name. When dry, however, slickrock can be extremely tacky and not very forgiving. Your footfall sounds like the endless scraping of sandpaper and your feet inside your shoes, sensing the tension of the hard slickrock, flex uncontrollably and uncomfortably with each step you take. Because of this, Jill developed a massive blister on the bottom of one of her feet about halfway through. It was dark by then, and I was pacing her. A minimal aid station crew was huddled around a fire. They didn't have a first aid kit, but they did have a knife and some duct tape. We used both. I lanced Jill's blister with the knife and then slapped duct tape over it for protection. My wife didn't complain. "Can we get out of here soon?" she asked, the minimal aid station crew not providing a lot of energy or support.

Jill ran a little bit ahead of the cutoffs as the sun rose and throughout the morning. The race had a 36-hour cutoff, and with about 20 miles to go, Jill began to lean forward. Her core muscles had taken an incredible pounding on the many climbs and on the challenge of the slickrock, and now they revolted, refusing to support her upper torso. With each mile, Jill began to lean forward more noticeably. She was using trekking poles, and with five miles to go, I thought the poles in her hand made her look like a hunched-over lobster. With each step she would take, now completely bent at the waist and hardly able to see in front of her, her poles would lash out at the ground, trying to pinch the red Martian-like dirt hard enough to propel her forward for a few yards. I was in the same hospital room with Jill when she gave birth to both Annie and Katie. Those were both physical feats that no one could ever equal. The pain of both of those labors, both of which pretty much started one day and finished the next as she brought forth life from her own body, looked like they hurt like hell. This ability to create something through such excruciating and prolonged pain was on my mind as I watched Jill struggle through those final few miles at Zion. She always completed everything she had ever started, and she had never complained, and this was way she finished Zion. Her back had to have put her in agony. The mere fact that she was lobstering along with her poles as cars drove up and down the highway leading us back into the small town of Virgin, Utah, some honking their encouragement and cheering wildly out their open windows for Jill to "Get 'er done!" had to have been both uplifting and deflating.

But then as she made her way into Virgin's tree-lined Town Park, something changed. Her posture improved. She wasn't completely upright. But she was no longer completely bent. She ran with a determined if not defiant pride that made it clear she was going to finish Zion on her terms. She crossed the finish line with her arms up, our friends from Reno who had run or paced the race that weekend descending on her like she had just scaled Everest. They hugged and kissed Jill, and Jill hugged and kissed them all back. She made her way to a fold-out chair, and the goodwill continued. My wife, who has always been there for so many other people over the years, was now the center of attention, and deservedly so. I remember standing there in the still-bright early evening of southern Utah thinking that Jill's 100-mile finish was the greatest 100-mile finish I'd ever seen in my life. I would never compare the enormity of giving birth to two daughters to what I witnessed in April 2015 with Jill's finish at Zion. But I will say this: It reminded me that as much as you have ever seen in your life, there is so much more that you will be gifted to see when you realize it is no longer about you but about others. The moment I experienced as I watched Jill finish her hundred-miler did what it was supposed to do. It pulled me from the narrowness of my own dreams, and it brought me into a new place, the wondrous dreams of others.

Run Your Race with an Open Heart

Everything finally came together for me more than eight years after my microfracture, during the first weekend of June 2015. Over the course of 22 hours and 35 minutes at that year's San Diego hundred-miler, I had a miraculous melding of my running past and my running present. They came together in a way that was unexpected yet entirely welcomed.

It was the dust and ash of old races once run replaced with the sun and light of a season still to come. It had been a full year since my last 100, which was also the San Diego 100. The day in 2014 had been hot, and though I managed to finish in a little under 25 hours, the race itself had been a succession of challenges—a touchy stomach early, a missed turn (all my fault) late that added a couple of miles. The wrong turn crushed me emotionally and left me struggling on the long climb up the relentless and rocky Stonewall Peak after mile 90 as dispirited as I'd ever been in a hundred. For a year, I'd dreamed and prepared for a return to San Diego, which is superbly RD'd by my dear friend, Scott Mills.

I told Jill before the race that I also wanted to run with an open heart. My best hundreds have always been those where I visit with my fellow runners, sharing small-talk, finding out a little something about them, and letting their personal race narrative become part of mine. And that was how the early miles played out. At the Paso Picacho aid station at mile seven, as we prepared to mount the boulder-laden, two-mile, 809-foot climb up Stonewall for the first time, I came across Scotty and his assistant RD, Angela Shartel. Scotty was shooting photos and smiling, shouting encouragement to me. Since we met on the Western States trail in a miraculous turn of fate in 2000 that saw Scotty literally pull me to my feet after I'd fallen, my friendship with him has been one of the defining relationships of my life. When we saw each other, the air became happily turbulent. Scotty and I immediately slapped joyful high-fives. I waved to Angela, and before I knew it, Angela stepped forward and enveloped me in a hug that I will always remember for its fierce protectiveness. Angela is a small woman, barely above five feet tall. Most who run against her are struck by her arms and her legs and her eyes. Her arms and legs are sculpted like precious metals. Her eyes shine like streaks of snow glistening in mountain sunlight.

"We were so happy that you came back to run our race again this year," Angela said, beaming.

"There's no way I'd miss it," I said. "I love your race!"

For the remainder of the race, it was that moment, seeing Scotty and his protégé, Angela—two people so rich in all that they have given, and all that they have gained—that would carry me forward.

As the heat of the day settled in, I had to remind myself to stay in the moment. Jill, Annie, and Katie had crewed me at the Pioneer Mail aid station at about 28 miles and would be waiting for me at the Meadows aid station at mile 51. I was excited to see them again, to share with them the ease with which the race was coming. About a half-mile from the Meadows at mile 51, well before the hustle and bustle of the aid station, I saw Jill along a fence line. She had walked out to greet me. For some reason, the sight of her, fresh off her own first 100-mile finish at Zion only two months earlier, filled me with a sense of shared experience. Jill had been my crew chief for all of my previous 12 hundred-milers, but this was the first one where she, too, was a 100-mile finisher herself. Seeing her along the fence line, waiting expectantly and then waving excitedly as I waved to her, made the late afternoon light go soft, more bearable, sanding down the edges of a hot day. We were now both 100-mile runners, and as we hugged, I could sense Jill knew exactly what it felt like to be more than halfway done with the journey.

Annie took on pacing duties at Penny Pines at mile 56. The 16-mile Noble Canyon/Pine Creek loop is easily my favorite part of the SD 100 course. It's a loop of contrasts. The first eight miles is all downhill to Pine Creek and does not play to my strengths at all. As I've aged, downhill running has become more of a pain. Yet I love the mini-ecosystems one passes through on this stretch; tall grasses give way to pine trees, which give way to a tightly tree-hemmed trail/slalom where dry leaves crackle impatiently under your footsteps, beckoning you to run faster. At the bottom near Pine Creek, the trail grows increasingly rocky, and cacti make their prickly appearance. And then there is the eight-mile climb out, back to Pioneer Mail at mile 72. Annie and I ran stretches where the climb would bottom out and then settle into a relentlessly strong hike. In contrast to the year before, we did not turn on headlamps until we were nearly four miles into the climb out. We were moving and moving well. At one point, we both turned and stared behind us as the far-off sky turned pink, then orange, then a fishnet of blazing red. "It's beautiful," I said. "You're doing so great!" Annie cheered. The mountain we were climbing was lumbering into its night sleep. And beneath her headlamp's light, Annie's blade-like face positively beamed, a fluorescent axis of eyes, nose, and mouth that were like life-filled sprinkles. I surprised myself with how strongly I power-hiked this section.

After running from Pioneer Mail to Sunrise and mile 79 by myself on the Pacific Crest Trail, Katie then took me home. I had been vaguely aware that there weren't all that many 50ish-year-olds near me for most of the day, and Katie, ever the ultra-geek who can dial up ultralive.net runner tracking updates quicker than atomic particles can bounce around a reaction chamber, had the immediate data for me after I hugged Jill and Annie good-bye at Sunrise. "I think you were right with another 50 at Sunrise," Katie said, the words spilling forth excitedly. "I think he's right behind us."

For the next hour, we worried less about the solo headlight of what turned out to be the very talented John Price behind us and concentrated instead on running efficiently with the climb up Stonewall still looming. The air chilled noticeably near the Chambers Landing aid station near mile 88, our breath floating through the air in ghost-like wisps. Stonewall awaited us. It would be about four miles to the top. For a time, I followed Katie's gentle strides, which carved their way with the grace of a young coyote through the tall, thick grasses of a meadow below the looming Stonewall.

Once the climb began, my stride took on more conviction than anything I had mustered all day. A year before, Stonewall had been like an unwelcome, demonic visitor. The rocky outcroppings, the constant stepping up and down over boulders, the sheer upward grade that made my legs feel like they were encased in cement had been like a constant, deflating knife to my resolve. I took the lead from Katie and did not let up. A year before, my hike had been little more than a sad slouch. As my weight shifted from one foot to another, I could feel myself narrow. All focus was simply, stubbornly, on the step I was yet to take. A serene detachment came over me as the earlier chill of Chambers and the meadow receded, replaced by the warmth of well-earned sweat. Flakes of dust and pebble and wood danced like sprites beneath my headlamp as we made our way to the top. "You're going to drop me, Daddy!" Katie called good-naturedly behind me at one point. We could no longer see the headlamps of anyone else on the switchbacks below. When we finally reached the top, my face eased into a smile. A rush of air met us, cool, stinging, and refreshing after the fevered intensity of the climb. Without realizing it, I had wandered into deeply unfamiliar territory. I suddenly felt like the runner I had once been. My memory hesitated. For a moment, there was a dull panic. Had I overdone it on Stonewall? Had the beautiful drudgery of the climb done me in? Had I sought out something I could no longer attain? Was the price of years too great? Did I have enough left to make it to the finish? Had I ruined my race chasing a younger version of myself?

The answer to all: No.

I won't lie. The final seven miles were not easy. Katie had to use all of her marvelous skills as a pacer to keep me dancing across the incredibly rocky final few miles. I nearly fell eight times over the last two miles. Yet, it was all strangely beautiful. As gingerly as we moved, in my mind's eye, it felt strong and coordinated. I was light-footed with every trip. Dancer-like spins and Gregory Hines-like tap-dance recovery answered every near-face plant. I was quietly smiling and non-fussy inside as I cursed the rocks aloud. For every pushback of the challenging trail, there was a sense of common ground, of growing internal strength and confidence as my body waned. There were also apparitions in the dark as we moved. My mind darted back in time to those runs with Lon at Virginia Lake during the winter of 2007-2008 when he showed me what friendship looked like. When he showed me that even if you are struggling, if your friend is still moving and is making progress, then what else is there in the world that really matters? And then everything fast-forwarded, from those first uneasy steps after my microfracture to where I had been that day. The San Diego 100 course reminds you just how long life can be. There are sections where you wind along Pacific Crest Trail, high above desert floor on one side and pine trees and manzanita on the other. You see the occasional PCT pilgrim as you run, their long journey having just begun a few days earlier at the Mexico-California border. Their stoic steadiness is a reminder that on the boulder-strewn trail, which shifts in color constantly from the permanence of russet to the color of dreams, of gold, you will find visions and ghosts of life that was lived and life that is still to be lived. There is a sense of long-ago and here-and-now, of struggle and redemption, of ways you have disappointed and the hope of making amends and finding a truer purpose. And from this land that seems so hard and unforgiving on its surface, so unbearably hot during the day, so tangled with boulders, you can still find hints of promise, of surprising beauty that feels like it belongs in a different, more heavenly place. It was in the tangle of boulders earlier, just before the sun had set, before Annie and I had reached the bottom of the canyon, where there was green shrub and the cool of a few oak trees. How could this be? How could there be so many trees that spoke of life in such an inhospitable place? The unfathomable mystery of it all had entranced me, reminded me that I was old, and I had lost things. But it reminded me, too, that as you grow old and lose things, there is always the potential to gain something new—a new perspective, a new understanding, a new way of relating to myself as a person and as a runner. Time had marched on, yet I was a still a runner. I no longer felt beholden to memory. What was in the past would not sustain me going forward. It had been eight years since my microfracture, and I finally needed to let some of that experience go. I needed to strike out on a new path, one that promised new adventures, new memory. It was the continued mystery of life that I wished to pursue.

And then my mind's reverie ended. A run across the highway. A quick dip into the coolness of the grassy field we had run across at morning's light some 22 hours and change earlier. Scotty's voice calling from the darkness, his voice full of emotion: "Is that John Trent? Is that John Trent? It's John Trent!"

Seeing the outline of the PVC pipe holding the SD 100 banner at the finish. The red lights of the race clock next to the banner, like the eyes of a fox peering at me with approval and grudging respect from the challenge of the darkness: 22:35.

"Just like the old days, Scotty," I called to Scotty as I followed Katie across the finish line. I thrust my fist into a star-filled sky. "Just like the old days!"

And then I was wrapped in Scotty's arms. It was an embrace I will never forget. As I buried my head in Scotty's shoulder, I knew suddenly I felt very rich. Rich for all that Scotty's special race had given me. And rich for knowing that for one day at least, the runner I once was had finally met and made peace with the runner I am now.

CHAPTER 9

The Magic of the
Golden Hour

It was late June in 2019, and my phone conversation with Jim Walmsley that day was like all of the conversations I'd ever previously had with him. Jim was just two days removed from winning his second straight Western States Endurance Run title, having improved his own course record of the year before to 14:09.

Like all of our conversations when I had interviewed Jim about his Western States experience for the long-form feature story I traditionally write for *Ultra Running Magazine* following Western States, Jim was candid, detailed with his memory, surprisingly humorous, self-effacing, serious, and pensive. Of all the great runners I've had a chance to interview in more than 35 years of being a journalist, Jim has always been at the top of my list for his willingness, whether he has succeeded or he has failed, to always share his thoughts on what happened. It's always easy when you've succeeded at the highest levels of athletics to "do" media and answer any and all questions about your unquestioned greatness. Jim has always held himself to a higher standard than most high-level athletes, however. He's experienced his share of failure. It happened once during his 2016 Western States debut when Jim had the race and a new course record locked up with 10 miles to go. But he then took a wrong turn and went horribly off course for several miles before he had to disconsolately retrace his wrong-way steps back on course before he walk-jogged with his family to the finish in 18th place. Even in moments of failure, I can't recall him ever ducking an interview request, which would have been easy to do. I still remember our phone conversation two days after his wrong turn. Jim was waiting for a ride. He was in a friend's Lake Tahoe garage. He said he had five minutes before his ride out of town showed up. He ended up giving me nearly 45 minutes. I told him at one point that I thought what had captured people's attention wasn't necessarily that he had appeared like a streaking meteor two days before, seemingly out of nowhere, running with a bold abandon that felt like ultra running had finally and suddenly discovered its Steve Prefontaine, but that he had shown he was human like all of the rest of us. He had made a mistake we could all relate to—a wrong turn late in a race. And instead of just giving up when he realized the race and the course record were lost, he had chosen to walk back over the same ground where he had made his mistake, back on course and back to the finish line. Jim hadn't chosen to drop out. He finished. Jim gave my statement a long and thoughtful pause. "Yeah, it's important to always see whatever you start through to the finish. That's life, right?" he said. And then he paused, adding with a light laugh, "And it was a good thing I turned around and walked to the finish, or else I might still be running in that wrong direction I took."

When I spoke to Jim in 2019, our conversation centered on a race that might've been the most well-executed in Western States' long history. His 14:09 course record was a near-flawless run by a runner in his late 20s who was at or near the height of his prodigious talents, who understood Western States' course the way a neuroscientist understands the human mind. There was nothing about the landscape that was inherently surprising to him. Yet Jim had maintained the wonder of the explorer entranced by the possibilities of the trail he ran over that day, feeling his experience deepening, his connection with the trail still growing and evolving with every stride he took.

"It's always been one step at a time for me," Jim said during our phone conversation after the 2019 race. "When these days happen, you really cherish it, knowing it may not happen again. Eventually, there will be a last one, so you've got to cherish these special, magical moments. They don't last forever."

Bookended with Jim's 14:09 course record in 2019 was what we witnessed during the final, desperate seconds of the race. Western States' 30-hour cutoff is christened during the race's final hour. When the clock hits 29 hours and there is an hour to go, the hundreds in attendance in the stands at Placer High School and the thousands watching live throughout the world via the race's livestream are given the treat of witnessing what is known throughout ultra running as the "Golden Hour." Over the final hour at Western States, runners of every conceivable shape, size, background, ability level, and gender begin to flow onto the Placer High School track as the ultimate embodiment of the human race. Some started out too fast and blew up. Others knew they would have to pace themselves due to lack of training or an injury and had doled out their effort like the most precious of natural recourses throughout the 100 miles and had timed their finish in such a way as to arrive at Placer High School relatively unscathed and relatively upright, in time for that final golden hour. Still others had fought throughout the blistering heat of the day and the doubt of the night and had struggled through cutoffs at aid stations throughout their Western States races like battered prize fighters who refused to go down. Some were covered completely in the orange dirt and dust of the trail and looked like they had been thrown out of the back of a moving bus. They wore the trail because they never had the luxury to stop and slow down and clean it off with a clean sponge or wet towel. There wasn't time for that for most of the runners who ran during the Golden Hour. They had to keep moving or else lose the battle of the clock and time out. There was a saying that some spectators wore on T-shirts at the finish line: "No Sleep 'til Auburn." Many of the runners who made the track in time for the Golden Hour knew firsthand what those words had meant, and how they had run through their own fatigue, pain, and inner demons to make it in time for one final Golden Hour lap on the Placer High School track. That last lap for the Golden Hour runners is something that we should all witness at least once in our lives. These runners were chosen in the Western States lottery from the more than 7,000 names from around the world who enter ultra running's most well-known lottery each year some seven months earlier. When they arrived at the track during the final hour of a historic race that spanned a couple of generations of runners, it was time to celebrate, to cheer, and to cry. The trail they had traveled had been much harder than they had planned, making their Golden Hour moment much sweeter than they could have ever anticipated.

And more than 15 hours after Jim Walmsley had run through the finish line with his arms raised and the crowd on its feet, there was less than a minute remaining when the final runner of the 2019 Western States sprinted toward that same finish line. At 29 hours and 59 minutes and one second, it was believed that Heather McGrath, a 44-year-old from Portland, Oregon, had been the final finisher. But then suddenly an expectant roar was heard just outside the stadium. Through the green stadium gate and onto the track swooped 47-year-old Lane Shimonishi of Honolulu, Hawaii followed by 25-time Western States finisher and five-time race champion Tim Twietmeyer. Over the years, Tim has made it his custom to run out from the stadium and get back on the trail for a few miles until he finds the last runner on the course who still had a chance of finishing in under 30 hours and then guides them home. Now, he was running next to Shimonishi, exhorting him on with yells of "You can do this! You can do this! You can do this!" Shimonishi was wearing a powder blue shirt and black sweats. The black sweats were a product of a night that had felt decidedly colder than the tradewind evenings of his native Hawaii. Running with all of his might to stay ahead of the race's cutoffs, Shimonishi never had the luxury of taking his sweats off once the sun had risen. "I felt like I was running for my life after the river," Shimonishi said of the race's final 22 miles after the Rucky Chucky crossing of the American River at mile 78. Shimonishi's hair was dark with sweat. He pumped his arms furiously as he sprinted toward the finish line. There were perhaps a little more than a thousand people on hand, many in the stands and hundreds crammed in at the finish line. But their collective screams and cheers of encouragement for Shimonishi felt like the stadium was entirely packed. As Shimonishi sprinted, the din rose like a massive wave. He crossed the finish line with his hands held in triumph in the air. Then he crumpled to the ground, completely spent. Longtime Western States board of trustees member Mark Falcone walked up to Shimonishi. Falcone bent his 6-foot-3 frame as low as he could go and wrapped a Western States finisher's medal around Shimonishi's neck. "You made it," a smiling Falcone told Shimonishi, taking Shimonishi's hand in his own and holding it for a moment in a mixture of awe and deep respect. "You made it to Auburn." Shimonishi had finished with 22 seconds to spare, in 29:59:38.

Shimonishi would later say that his mantra throughout the entire race, even when he was exhausted and his prospects for a finish appeared to dim, was simple.

"Today is not the day to stop," he said.

To reach the Golden Hour, no truer words could ever be spoken. Especially when you consider that once Lane Shimonishi crossed the finish line in 2019 at Western States, he would remain the very last person to do so for two long years as the pandemic raged and the race was cancelled in 2020. Jim Walmsley was right. We always need to cherish these most special and magical moments. They don't last forever. They may not ever happen again.

Find Your Own Golden Hour

Why is the golden hour so special? Why is it, in the words of Tony Rossmann, a past president of the event, "the finest hour in all of ultra running," and why do those final few finishers of the event tell us so much about who we are? A few years ago when I was writing about Jim Walmsley's excellence at Western States, I likened what he did to the old Thornton Wilder play, *Our Town*. Of all the universal themes of *Our Town*, the one that has always stuck with me over the years is the notion that we aren't always aware of many of the most pivotal moments in our life until often it is too late to glean any lasting meaning from them. Decisions are made and directions are set in our lives, often without realizing that there might've been earlier moments that, if we had given their proper illumination and importance, might've set us on an entirely different direction after we had made entirely different decisions. Wilder writes at one point, "We can only be said to be alive in those moments when our hearts are conscious of our treasures." I had written this in *Ultra Running Magazine* as it related to how Jim Walmsley, over the course of his career at Western States, had in his brilliance ("Course record!") and in his imperfection ("Wrong turn!") had caught the imagination and the earned the admiration of the people of Auburn. I think, too, that the runners of the Golden Hour at Western States deserve this type of special designation. The final finishers at Western States are well aware of the incredible sacrifice they have made in order to reach the finish line. Their hearts are entirely conscious of the treasure that is before them as they run those final few yards on the Placer High School track a little bit before an air horn blasts at exactly 11 a.m. on Sunday, signifying that an event that had started 100.2 miles away at 5 a.m. the previous day had finally, officially, concluded for the year.

The Golden Hour represents our finest hour because of the people who become a part of it. Some are among the finest athletes in the race, but most aren't. They are more like Lane Shimonishi, a quiet but very thoughtful tax auditor for the State of Hawaii who's also a father of three and the type of person who will let you know that if you are ever in Hawaii, you have to call him so that he can host you and take you on a run so that he can show off the wonders of Honolulu and the surrounding area's trails. "Let me know if you are ever in Hawaii," he will say. "We should go for a run."

Shimonishi ran Western States unlike most runners, who run with a pacer over the final 38 miles. He chose to run alone. He was in awe of Western States' beauty from the start, including the "High Country" section of the first 16 or so miles. Whenever the Sierra Nevada has a good snow year—and 2019 was one of those years—this section often remains under snow.

"For me, as a local boy from Hawaii, I had never trained on or ran in snow," he admitted. "I was a little scared about it at first. But it turned out to be one of the highlights for me. It just felt so cool—the different textures, slipping and falling a couple of times—and sometimes, not by mistake, falling. It was fun."

Though he ran without a pacer, Shimonishi said he never felt alone. Western States has more than 1,500 volunteers, most of whom are extremely enthusiastic about the race. Western States volunteers have a reputation for going beyond in everything they do. They fill bandanas with ice on hot days. They help the runners apply cold, wet sponges to their legs. They clean wounds. They mend shattered running ego with praise and a smile. "The volunteers were the best," Shimonishi said. "They got me to think about nothing else but getting to the finish. They kept me motivated and pushed me, which was great."

Shimonishi remembered the scene at Robie Point, which marks the end of the trail at a trailhead at the far end of one of the oldest neighborhoods in Auburn. There are only 1.3 miles left at that point. The volunteers at Robie Point were running down the long, steep climb to their aid station, meeting the final runners first a quarter mile, then a half mile, away from their aid station, tossing cold towels on the runners' shoulders, squeezing every last ounce of water out of their sponges on the runners' necks, encouraging them to not give up, to keep driving for the finish line. Shimonishi found their whole-hearted willingness to give inspiring. "How many times in your life do you have that kind of support?" he asked. "It was kind of overwhelming to think that it was directed towards me, to help me, to get me to the finish. The goodness of people . . . how can you put it into words when you experience it like that?"

"I surprised myself," he said. "You just kind of forget about everything else. The only thing that matters is getting to the finish."

And then Shimonishi allowed himself a gentle chuckle.

"I didn't realize it was going to be that close," he said.

"I Can Only Do It in This Life"

Helga Backhaus was without question one of the most accomplished ultra marathoners of the 1990s. Her record of achievement at Western

States was so consistent that it almost become a foregone conclusion: She would travel to America in June from Germany each year, and she would finish in the top 10 of the women's race. She would do so with a warm smile and never-ending sense of appreciation directed toward all who were involved with Western States. "Helga is just pure class," the late Western States race director Greg Soderlund once said of her. "Nobody does it quite the way she does. I don't know if there is a happier or more optimistic elite runner out there than her." Helga finished among the top 10 women in nine of her races, including finishing second in 1995, the legendary "Ice and Fire" year where the course had more than 24 miles of snow and temperatures later in the day that soared above 100 degrees. But shortly after her ninth finish (all of which had been under 24 hours) in 2001, Helga was seriously injured, when she was hit by a car while on a bike. She spent the next four years recovering from a severe leg injury and nine agonizing surgeries.

She returned to Western States in 2005. She ran a race that kept her near the cutoffs but never behind them. At each aid station, even as she ran with a slight limp, she greeted all of the volunteers as they had always been to her—as family. As she made her way up to the Placer High track from Robie Point, her 10th finish now in reach, volunteers, onlookers, and friends began to follow behind her. With her glasses and her ready smile, the 52-year-old looked like she was a teacher leading a group of students on a field trip. She hurried around the track with a series of short strides that, although they looked clipped and tired, were also full of the momentum of what was about to happen. The crowd in the stands rose to its feet as she finished in 29:58:09. She told Greg Soderlund before the race that even with her injury, "Our greatest deeds can always still be in reach."

A year later, Western States honored Helga by using a photo of her from the 2005 race—her 10th finish—on the cover of its printed race program. Helga wrote an email of thanks to those of us who were on the board of trustees at the time.

It read in part:

"The WS 100 was and still is, and will always be, a big part of my life!

. . . And now I'm on the cover of the greatest 100-mile race in the world!
What an honour!!! I can't believe it!! It makes me so very proud and happy!!

It was so very, very hard, to come back after the bike/car accident, to learn walking again and then tried to find out how I can use the remaining lower leg for running again. Sometimes I was crying, because, it seems impossible to use it ever again. . . . But deep in my mind and heart, I knew, I'll run again one day. And I must do my number 10 WS100. I can do it only in this life!
. . . And all the months in hospitals, suffering and surviving 9 surgeries . . . didn't know if I'll leave hospital with two legs. I had this big dream! I was sure! Doctors and professors thought, I'm a poor, crazy one!

Thinking back, it was like a really bad dream, a nightmare!

Now I'm very, very happy!
Thank you very much for everything you had done for me.
And that you let me come back, doing number 10!
Maybe, when I applied, you thought, "She is crazy, that she is running without the Achilles tendon and with only 30 percent of

muscles in the lower leg. But you gave me this chance! You believed in
me! Thank you sooooooo very much!

Very good to know that I've got very, very good friends in
California! I'm thinking of number 11 one day!

Now I'm back to 18 km in 2:10 hours and feeling good again (just
some little problems, which I always will have).
In December, I'll go to the Honolulu Marathon. Just to do something
special this year and enjoy two weeks of sunshine and this beauti-
ful scenery and enjoy the Marathon. If I'm not really ready for this
Marathon, there is enough time to walk it!

I'm wishing you all the very best . . . the very, very best!
Stay healthy and "Happy Trails!"

Lots of greetings to you all and everybody who remembers me,
Helga

Lane Shimonishi said, "Today is not the day to stop" for his Golden
Hour finish. Helga's words were just as moving and meaningful. Our
hearts must always be conscious of our treasures. Or as she put it so
eloquently about the time we are given in our lives to do the things that
matter most: "I can do it only in this life."

Outrunning the Clock

Like Jim Walmsley, Rob Krar's championship connection with Western
States says a great deal about what kind of person Rob is. Rob showed
up from his home in Flagstaff at Western States in 2013 wearing a
straw cowboy hat and a long, brown beard, possessing some intriguing

running credentials. Growing up in Canada, he excelled in triathlon and during his collegiate running career, Rob nearly broke four minutes in the mile. He competed in road racing for a while, but injuries necessitated a change, so he moved to ultras and trail running. He finished second to Timothy Olson in 2013, then resoundingly won Western States in 2014 and 2015. What set Rob apart wasn't necessarily his fast running but his self-awareness. He had battled depression for a significant portion of his life. He had struggled through times when he would be practically paralyzed by it. Western States provided Rob with an opportunity to realize his talent and use that talent to seek out a competitive dream. It also gave him the opportunity to share his story in a public forum among the people who over a three-year period he had grown to know, trust, and call his friends. Prior to his win in 2015, Rob, with only a few handwritten notes to work from, was one of the presenters during a medical conference that was held in conjunction with that year's Western States. He spoke openly and candidly about his depression, how it affected him as a young man and how, now in his mid-30s, it had continued to be a part of his life as a husband and as an elite athlete. "It was a great talk just because it was just so open and honest about what Rob had always felt," Dr. Andy Pasternak, Western States' medical director, said. "You could tell that Rob is the type of person who sees this as more than something that's about himself. He has a way of reaching out and wanting to help others through his example and through what he has experienced."

Rob and his wife, Christina, had made their way out to the Robie Point neighborhood the morning after he'd won Western States in 2015. They wanted to see the Golden Hour runners make their way to the finish and experience the energy of those who were cheering them on. The dozens upon dozens of people they saw sitting in the yards and on the street of the neighborhood did not disappoint. It felt as if a high school football game was running right through the middle of the street, and like an entire small town had shown up to see it, with colorful banners and signs in the yards and some cheering sections on some corners of some homes stretching two or three deep. Rob was wearing his trademark straw cowboy hat. He was giving his blistered feet a break by wearing a pair of flip flops. A few of the Robie Point partiers recognized him: "Hey, there's the guy who won Western States!" or "Hey, Rob!" He visited with them, thanked them, and joined in on their cheering as the 29-hour runners. With their pacers, crews, and families all in tow and exultant that there was still time left before the finish, the Golden Hour runners ran by the crowd with happy waves.

As the time compressed and the cutoff time inched closer, there was less merriment and more purposeful effort. There were only 10 minutes to go now and a little more than a mile left to run. That was about the time Katie, who was running her first hundred-miler that day, with me serving as her pacer, ran by Rob and Christina and all the Robie yard parties. Katie had battled cutoffs since the 47-mile mark at Devil's Thumb. Her worst nightmare hadn't been the heat, the terrible canyon climbs, or even the mounting fatigue of running one hundred miles. It had been the sound of air horns blowing. At each aid station, as the final cutoff time expired, an air horn would pierce the air with an awful finality. If you weren't at the aid station yet where the air horn sounded, you were disqualified and couldn't run on. If you were just out of the aid station where the air horn sounded, the grim reality was that you would need to run as hard as you possibly could in order to get in and out of the next aid station before the air horn wound sound again. It was as if the grim reaper had begun trailing you and was waiting for you to demonstrate a weakness that you had always hoped hadn't been residing inside of you. Katie was 22 years old and had never faced this kind of enormous pressure in her running life. When I began pacing her at the Highway 49 crossing with a little more than six miles to go, I told her, "Honey, you're basically going to have to run every step of the way from here to the finish in order to finish in under 30 hours." Katie nodded, and then set out to do just that. By the time we ran by Rob and Christina, we had seen Tim Twietmeyer on his journey out from the track to welcome the last few lucky souls back to Auburn. Tim had given us the thumbs up and then ran with us for a several hundred yards. "You're not going to crack, Katie," he told Katie as he turned to see if there was anyone else out there still running with a chance at breaking 30 hours.

Tim was right. Katie didn't crack. She finished in 29 hours, 56 minutes, and 34 seconds. She was immediately enveloped in jubilant friends and family who were experiencing the happiest waterworks imaginable. I think the only other time in my life I've ever cried more about her was the day she was born. And then, there was an expectant hush as the clock wound down. Another runner, John Corey of Cincinnati, came barreling down the track and finished in 29:59:27.

Was there anyone else out there?

There was. Gunhild Swanson, a 70-year-old grandmother from Spokane Valley, Washington, was nearing the final 100 meters. Gunhild was a remarkable athlete who had completed more than 200 races ranging from marathons to 100-milers over the previous four decades. She had started running in 1977 because she thought she needed to be in better shape as she approached middle age. During her race in 2015, she had actually gone off course for a while due to a directional error while she was being paced by her grandson. Katie remembered going back and forth with Gunhild at various points in the race and was impressed by how strongly Gunhild hiked all of the climbs, which shouldn't have been surprising since Gunhild had been an avid hiker with her late husband.

Rob saw Gunhild not long after Gunhild left the trail and touched the Robie Point pavement. He was still feeling the effects of his winning run and had sort of hobbled throughout the neighborhood earlier. But seeing Gunhild sparked something in him. As she ran by, hustling along on a steep uphill, half-running, half-power-hiking, he jumped in next to her. He didn't quite know why. He offered her words of encouragement, as did many others who had also joined Gunhild at this point. When they hit a couple of the long downhills, he could hear his flip-flops slapping crazily, almost out of control, against the asphalt.

"I just got so caught up in it," he told me later, when I interviewed him about his victory. "It was such an amazing moment. Here was this incredibly strong woman, giving it her all. There was this voice in my head that told me that it wasn't a great idea to jump in with her. What if she didn't make it? What if she came up short and just missed it?

"But I couldn't help myself. In a strange and really wonderful way, I was sort of reliving my run through the same neighborhood from the night before. You don't know about these special, magical moments that really matter until they pop up right before you. And when they do, you want to know that you embraced them and didn't miss them.

"The energy of that moment was pretty overpowering to me. I wanted Gunhild to get to that finish line just like I had."

Over the final 100 meters. Gunhild ran with a slightly bent-at-the-waist but highly effective and quick turnover. She claimed later that she possessed no finishing kick, no semblance of a sprinter's ample fast-twitch muscles. The results, however, told a different story. Gunhild could sprint with the best of those who belonged to the Golden Hour. She finished in 29:59:54. With just six seconds to spare, Gunhild had become the oldest woman to ever finish Western States. Just about three minutes earlier, the race's youngest finisher that year, 22-year-old Katie Trent of Reno, Nevada, had also finished. Age and youth had both been served that morning. It had been a grandmother and a girl young enough to be her granddaughter who had sent the Placer High School crowd into a frenzy. It was a widow and a young woman yet to be married who had reminded everyone of why, when life's most precious memories pass before us, we must seize them with everything we possess.

"I was just in awe of the strength that Gunhild ran with," Rob Krar said. "She was going to make it to the finish line no matter what."

The finest hour in ultra running had worked its Golden Hour magic yet again.

CHAPTER 10

Salvation in **the Bighorns**

I've reached the point in my running life where it is inevitable to feel on occasion that the road seldom traveled can feel like the road often traveled. We accumulate so many miles, races, and experiences through-out a calendar year that if we are not careful, a laconic complacency can take over what we do. The unexpected becomes the expected. The new becomes the old. Running 100 miles, strangely, can sometimes seem, if you do it often enough, like not that big a deal. When I traveled to the Bighorn hundred-miler in Dayton, Wyoming along with Jill and Katie, on June 15, 2016, there was a lot working against me. I'd over-come a blown calf from late in 2015 to resume running again. I had actually developed a decent base of fitness into May. Then, the day after race-directing and then pulling ribbon for our hometown ultra, the Silver State 50/50, my knee locked on me. It was painful enough that Jill had to pick me up after I had trudged dispiritedly for eight miles off Peavine Mountain.

For the next month, I ran very little. My good friend and a local doctor, Derek Beenfeldt, took a look at the knee and suggested more rest and a gradual return to running. A hundred-mile runner himself, Derek didn't rule out running Bighorn, which I was grateful to hear. I'd been down this road before, with an assortment of injuries over the past several years, and like a drunk with an open tab at the local bar, I made my way to my physical therapist, Michael Spevak. I'd visited Michael's bright and airy office in west Reno so many times over the past few years, the receptionist, Sarah, recognized my voice immediately on the phone when I made the first of several PT appointments. "We don't ever want to say we're happy to see you again," Sarah said, "but you are one of our happier and more motivated patients." The cycle of rest, PT, ice, and a gradual return to running kicked in. Luckily, it seemed to work. Eventually the pain subsided in my knee. I committed to run Bighorn just a few days before it was to be held.

I was going off to run in Wyoming—a place I'd never run before. Yet, the road to that point—an injury, PT, and a gradual return to running— had felt familiar to me.

Quickly, though, the trip to Bighorn began to feel different. Like three freshmen on our first weekend away from home at college, we stayed in a five-room residential suite at Sheridan College, about 20 miles from the start/finish in Dayton. For the price of a regular hotel room, Jill, Katie, and I had full run of a space that was well over 1,000 square feet, with washer/dryer, full kitchen, three bathrooms, and a wrap-around porch where we would sit in the evening as Sheridan's warm weather would become cool and inviting.

We loved Sheridan. The locals held a street party on Thursday night, complete with country western music, food, drink, and booths that I think summed up the melodic contrasts that make Wyoming such an emotionally resonant place: plentiful green and yellow John Deere machinery on display, followed by exquisite arts and crafts created in the hues of the state: brown and peach pottery, oil paintings of wide-open blue skies, and deep green hillsides and mountaintops.

In all of my years of ultra running, I had never run a hundred-miler that started so late in the morning. The 11 a.m. start on Friday, June 17 was preceded by a 9 a.m. trail briefing at the finish in Dayton. Race director Michelle Maneval kept things positive and fun. Her mother, Karen Powers, a wiry, gray-haired woman with a ready smile and one of the run's original founders, stood nearby. In the days leading up to the run, Karen, who in 2016 was in her late 60s, had been out marking major sections of the course. She would be a constant presence at the finish line and would be one of the people who would drape a cooling wet towel around my shoulders and hug me once I crossed the finish line. As Michelle asked us all to applaud the more than 300 volunteers, including more than 120 search-and-rescue workers who would be staffing aid stations (of the 13 aid stations, six of them were so far off the beaten track, supplies had to packed in on horse a few days earlier), I glanced at her mother, who beamed with pride.

"We have the best volunteers," Michelle said. "It's very rewarding for them. They are helping you achieve a dream, which you've all had for a very long time and have trained very hard for. But it takes a lot of behind-the-scenes support. These are the people who want nothing more than to see you reach your goal.

"This place means so much to all of us. And we want to share it with all of you."

Running as Resistance

Back in the late 1980s, a hydroelectric project was planned for the area. The project would have had dire consequences for the canyons leading up from Dayton into the passes and peaks of the Bighorn Range. So, a group of residents, including Karen Powers, decided to fight back by creating the Bighorn trail runs in 1993, which originally included 30K, 50K, and 50-mile distances. The hundred-miler was added in 2002. Their reasoning for the runs was simple. The more people who saw the beauty of the Bighorns, where all manner of wildlife, from moose to elk to deer frolic, and where wild and scenic rivers like the Dry Fork and the Little Bighorn run with such untrammeled purity and lifeforce they seem to rise out of the pages of a Jim Harrison novel, the more who wouldn't want a hydroelectric project ruining such a beautiful place. The Bighorn Trail Runs have been a two-day celebration of running and a resounding success. The public awareness Karen and her race organizers created mushroomed into united opposition to the project. Eventually, plans for the project died (though the Bighorn website warns that development is a constant threat).

"The Dry Fork project would've put a hydroelectric dam in a place that was very wild and scenic—a place that very few people knew about," Michelle said. "We just wanted to raise awareness."

Bighorn's race organization is emblematic of the amazing things people are capable of doing, particularly when they feel their race is in their blood.

"Every family has a story," Michelle said. "Bighorn is a big part of ours."

As the Bighorn races evolved, it took an entire family, Karen Powers' family, to make it happen. Michelle Maneval, Karen's daughter, is not a runner. She jokes often that she leaves the running up to her adventurous and "bad-ass" mother. But ever since the first Bighorn was held on the first weekend in June in 1993, Michelle has known that Bighorn is more than just a race. It represents that first act of defiance by the running community that the natural habitat areas around the Dry Fork Drainage and Little Bighorn Rivers and their solemn beauty had to remain the way it has always been. The races, too, are about the tight and lasting bonds that can be formed when a community can come together. That it is her family (particularly the women of her family) that have been the driving force behind the Bighorn races for three decades makes Michelle proud, as well as protective, of the special experience that the races offer. Bighorn, in fact, is one of the few ultras in the entire country where the race management team is all women. Michelle is the race director; Karen is the course director; Michelle's aunt Cheryl Sinclair is the assistant race director; Melanie Green, Michelle's sister, is the medical and timing director. Whatever profit the race makes is donated to a host of local charities, including the Sheridan Area Search and Rescue.

"We're an all-women's team," Michelle said. "I think because of that fact, the emotion is different . . . how we approach the race and what we feel are the most important priorities can sometimes be different. We put runner well-being, safety, as well as a sense of belonging to some-thing bigger than yourself, above everything else.

"We all love our race so much, and it's such a part of us. It's a part of our being, and it's something much bigger than all of us. The commu-nity and the thing that it builds, the human spirit that you see, the community spirit and the volunteerism that it helps to build, it really is something special."

Michelle and Karen are two of the most successful business owners in Sheridan, located about halfway between Mount Rushmore and Yellowstone National Park, not far from the Montana border. They own four retail business on Main Street, including the Sport Stop, which Karen opened more than three decades ago as more of a racquetball/tennis shoe shop. Today it is one of the top outdoor shops of its kind in the region. Bighorn's success certainly can be traced to its all-women's management team, coupled with the experienced entrepreneurial business sense that Karen and Michelle have accrued over the years.

"The 'girl power' aspect of our race has been mentioned to me a few times over the years," Michelle said. "I haven't really thought about it a lot. But I would say that women are great planners . . . maybe men like to fly by the seat of their pants a bit more. But with the women, and I don't want this to sound sexist, there might more of a natural tendency to come together, to work together, as problem-solvers."

Karen agreed: "Maybe we don't have the egos others would. We all seem to know our roles. We are definitely there for each other."

There is one other thing, Michelle said, when asked about Bighorn's success. The entire community loves it.

"We have a small community," she said. "We have 18,000 people in our community. The people in our community, the volunteers, they love our event. I would think that over the past 28 years, a large number of the 18,000 people in our community have helped or volunteered with Bighorn in some way.

"Without our volunteers, Bighorn just doesn't happen."

Michelle is a woman who smiles and laughs easily. Throughout every Bighorn weekend, she sleeps very little and is on hand to congratulate every finisher at the cottonwood-lined finish line at Scott Park in nearby Dayton, Wyoming. When she speaks about her mother, there is a sense of pride and wonder. Karen Powers belongs to a different generation of ultra runners, among the first group of athletes who took on the challenge of long distance, found a calm sense of elegant simplicity in the struggle to go long distances, and made it part of who they were. Michelle can remember being in her early 20s and helping her mother in the early 1990s as Karen, then in her early 40s, heard the alluring siren call of the ultra scene and then ran of some of the first hundred-milers founded in North America: Wasatch, Leadville, and Angeles Crest.

"I do remember the first time I ever went for a run in the Bighorns," Karen said, in a voice that is wisdom personified: thoughtful, careful, and soft, the way any runner who has something to say should sound. "I went with these friends of mine. It was a little group. I'd eaten a piece of toast that morning. I had no food during the run. We picked berries on the trail along the way. That helped keep me going. We went 19 miles that day."

Karen was like all of the most discerning ultra runners. Whenever she went for a run, she did so not just for the miles but for the experience, the sensation, and the emotion that can build as one covers territory in a picturesque place. The wondrous limestone cliffs of the Bighorns are certainly that as are its elk and its moose, and the unruly afternoon clouds, which can tilt your perception and make you question what you are seeing. The Bighorn mountains become like massive green boats sunken under a blue ocean that never ceases. Karen has loved every moment of her time spent there.

"To me, it's a very special place," Karen said. "It's almost spiritual to me in some ways."

Michelle never felt her mother was leaving her family behind when Karen would go out on her long training runs. To the contrary, she believed that Karen's never-ending search for hundred-mile finishes made her mother a better person—a person who was more acutely aware of the natural world and always willing, no matter who it was and how far they wished to travel, to share what she was experiencing in the Bighorns with them.

"My mom has been to places in those mountains that no one else has ever been," Michelle said. "She knows all the secrets of the Bighorn."

Michelle's teen-aged son, Noah, has run the Bighorn races several times himself. Michelle said that she can already see the next generation of the Powers/Maneval family about to take the reins of what is a community treasure.

"Noah has marked trail with my mom since he could walk," Michelle said. "Trail running has been in his blood. He's been born into it. Whenever I've seen him finish our race, crossing the same finish line as all the other runners we've welcomed over the years, coming around the corner into Scott Park, I know exactly how emotional it can be.

"Those tears really can flow when you see your runner finishing our race. It really is something, to see your runner come in off that river road and finish this incredible adventure they've been on in the Bighorn."

Letting Go and Opening Up

We gathered in the Tongue River Canyon for the start. We ran into Sophie Carpenter Speidel, who had traveled from her home in Virginia to support friends from the Virginia Happy Trails Running Club, as well as to run the next day's 52-miler. Sophie, whom I had met the year before at Western States, is an unforgettable presence. She has a face of intricate emotions and a manner that is all attention and tender sensibility, her words always informed with an uncommon decency. She's a lithe woman, and strong. She had run the race before and had fallen in love with it. "It's such a beautiful course," Sophie said. "You're going to love it."

The race began, and up the Tongue River trail we ran. I moved cautiously at first, testing my knee on the occasional rocky ups as we made the 3,450-foot climb that would stretch for the race's first 7.5 miles. This would prove to be a theme for the day, night, and the next day. Long climbs, followed by even steeper climbs, followed by long downhills, followed by even steeper downhills. As we ascended the canyon, the mountain grasses grew long, along with the wildflowers. I ran beside a Canadian runner, Larry Kundrik, who had run Bighorn five times, as well as Hardrock. Bespectacled and efficient, he moved with the economy of a seasoned mountain runner, his stride never too long, his effort never too rash, his words never too extravagant.

The hillsides of wildflowers, though, were the one exception.

"You think they're great now," Larry said, smiling back at me over his shoulder. "Wait until you see what comes later. Unlike anything you will ever see."

Larry was right. As we traveled into the Bighorns, the wildflowers seemed to flow in a contemplative slow motion that invited you to stare, all surprisingly tall and bright, yellow and purple and red, like the colors of a fair mountain maiden's sun dress. The day before, Jill, Katie, and I had scouted the course and had driven to the two aid stations where they would provide me crew support: mile 13.4 at Dry Fork Ridge and mile 48 at Jaws Trailhead, where Katie would then jump in and pace me for the final 52 miles. On our drive into Dry Fork, three black moose stood sentinel near the aid station (and a mud hole), unhurried and unfazed as we drove past them.

As I arrived at the bustling saddle at Dry Fork aid station, the moose from the day previous were gone, though Jill and Katie would later report they had seen more moose on their drive in. Gone, too, was my apprehension about my knee. It had held up well and would continue to hold up to the finish. This was good, because the next several miles were a rolling descent down a primitive jeep trail to the Cow Camp aid station near mile 20. For the first time, as we dropped more than a thousand feet, the cool mountain air shifted dramatically and began to feel warm. Highs on Friday would be in the 80s and were predicted to reach the high 90s the next day. I took advantage of the many streams lapping across the trail and wet my bandana and hat often.

A feature of the course that had piqued my curiosity was the so-called "Wall," a 2,000-foot descent in a little over three miles that occurred not long after I'd passed the marathon mark after 26 miles. At first, the Wall wasn't apparent. As I've grown older, I've found myself growing increasingly agitated with technical downhills. After leaving the Bear Hunting Camp aid station at mile 26, the trail immediately became divoted, full of deep, gray holes made from muddy hooves that had since dried. I cursed mildly under my breath as I side-stepped and tight-roped and slipped and nearly fell. I could feel my feet tensing inside my shoes, creating friction and heat (and, not long after, huge blisters on both my heels). Just when I began to question if I were ever going to escape the divot-land that had so thoroughly grabbed my attention and I began wondering if I would ever be allowed to gaze any further than six inches of front of my face, the trees around me quietly disappeared.

It was late in the afternoon, and the sky opened to a vast expanse of blue. A cool breeze brushed softly across my nose. The Wall revealed its secrets to me. I was on a ridgeline now, clearly viewing what was down below and up above. Down below was land tempered with green plains and far-off mountaintops that, together, seemed to roll on for miles. To my right were canyon walls that were khaki, peach, and orange, and were so formidable and awe-inspiring I thought that they must possess the strength of giants. I stopped dead in my tracks, no longer muttering or cursing, my head craned upward, captured by the beauty. The whole scene reminded me of holiness, of a timeless eternity—of a road and a place I'd never traveled before. I spent a reverent moment of silence, standing completely still, watching the slowly descending light of the day grow softer along the canyon walls, the ridgeline's wind sweeping tenderly and sweetly, like a long sigh, along my cheeks.

I grew emotional, and stayed that way, all the way down the rest of the Wall, to the Foot Bridge aid station at mile 30, which was located literally across a footbridge over the roaring Little Bighorn River. I was met by a young man who had my drop bag already ready, as dozens of other aid station volunteers scurried about, doing the same service for other runners. I saw the great Western States champion Pam

Smith, who had unfortunately decided to drop out. Only a few weeks before, Pam had run a remarkable track run, covering new American Record distances for 100 miles as well as 200 kilometers. Not surprisingly, at Bighorn, Pam was still feeling her superb run's affects. I've always admired Pam so much, for many reasons. She's accomplished, a seasoned healthcare professional and researcher, but she never puts on airs or acts accomplished. In fact, it is her self-deprecating, humorous nature that draws many of us to her. Still feeling the emotion of the Wall, I hugged Pam tightly after she told me about her race. In typical Pam fashion, she flashed me an upbeat smile and wished me well. I told her I was excited to meet my daughter, Katie, at Jaws, so Katie could pace me into the finish.

"You know, John, I really think it's so neat how you and your family do so many of these runs together," Pam, herself a mother of two, said. "That's such a great thing, to be able to share a run like this with your daughter."

Again, the emotions came. I left Foot Bridge feeling my heart swell and my throat tighten. Pam was right. I am such a lucky man.

The climb up to Jaws was 18 miles long and covered more than 4,000 feet. The Little Bighorn Canyon was densely forested, and it was difficult for a time to tell if it was getting dark or if the weather was changing. I heard a clap of thunder, then a few minutes later, another. As the canyon finally opened, a light rain fell for a few minutes. As I crossed a meadow near the 40-mile Spring Marsh aid station, it was nearing 9 p.m. A full moon was rising, and with it, the sky became veined with sharp, dramatic flashes of light, followed by more thunder.

"Great," I thought to myself. "I'm in a beautiful meadow in the middle of a lightning storm. Its beauty is going to kill me."

For the rest of the evening, the thunder and the lighting of the sky would continue, though it would drift like an echo off away from us, less of a threat and more of yet another wild and scenic feature of this wild and scenic run. Or as Katie would note, "This is just so cool!"

Jill and Katie were a welcome sight at Jaws, which was located off a dirt road at nearly 9,000 feet. The aid station featured a massive white circus tent, where runners sat in folding chairs, near a heater, with Led Zeppelin music blasting. I was in and out of the tent quickly, now 13 hours into the run, and moved a few hundred yards down the road to Jill and Katie and our rental car and my own personal aid station. It was chilly out, and as we talked, we could see our breath. Katie was dressed in a stocking cap, puffy jacket, and tights, and was excited to get going. Jill was patient, as she always is during my runs, and caring. The woman has an irrational fear that I am always cold in my ultras, particularly at night, and she made sure I had my gloves and an extra layer just in case the night grew colder. With a kiss, she sent Katie and I off from Jaws.

The 18 miles back down to Foot Bridge were fine at first, but gradually the downhill, the rockiness, and the occasional mud puddles that needed to be negotiated all took a toll. We reached Foot Bridge just after sun-up, 66 miles in, a little after 5 a.m.

"I'm worked," I told Katie as I slumped into a chair. An overwhelming sense of disappointment came over me; my pace had slowed, my blisters were becoming troublesome, and I was wondering if I still had a finish left within me.

"Don't worry, Daddy, you're doing fine," Katie told me. "You feel like you're slowing down, but you're really not. Don't get sad. Think about what a beautiful place this is and how well you've done. This is an incredible race. You're doing great!"

A volunteer gave me a safety pin, and I popped my blisters and changed shoes. Katie, who herself was eating an Egg McMuffin—the aid station was also known as "the McDonald's aid station"—began feeding me calories and liquid. After about 20 minutes, I was up again, and we began to trudge our way back up the Wall. As inspiring and emotionally moving as the Wall was on the way down, it seemed interminably tortuous on the way up.

Even Katie noticed the steepness.

"These people in Wyoming don't believe in switchbacks," she said. "Everything, every trail, is straight up."

After about 10 minutes, another runner, defeated by the Wall, was headed toward us, in the wrong direction, headed back to Foot Bridge to drop out.

"Have fun," he said, rolling his eyes as we continued on past him.

Eventually, as we neared the top of the Wall, I began to feel better. As the terrain leveled, we fell into a run/walk pattern. I followed Katie's lead. She'd hand me food and would begin running, gently, then more strongly, and I would follow. The calories were working. At one point, she handed me a piece of a Snickers bar and I devoured it practically before it was out of her hand.

Without realizing it, Katie had taken control of my run, and I was more than willing to let her do it.

By mile 80, we were back on pace, with a clear goal in mind: Break 30 hours.

Then the heat began to set in. As we made the long climb back up to Dry Fork at mile 87, Katie's puffy jacket had long been deposited into her pack. The long-sleeve shirt she had worn was now draped around her shoulders. The frequent streams on the climb saved us. We'd dip hats and bandanas and shirts in the cold water, talking at first, but gradually growing silent as the warm morning pressed its oppressive palm, frying-pan hard, to our faces. The heat began to bend me forward, imposing its will upon me. As much as I tried to straighten myself, its force just seemed too great.

Jill met us at Dry Fork, which felt infernal compared to the day before, when I had skipped through feeling so fresh. Some Coke and some watermelon helped me stand straighter. We were on the homestretch, and although my blisters hurt, I felt I was walking well and still capable of short bursts of running. The final nine miles proved challenging, however; much of the trail was steep downhill back into Upper Sheep Creek and the Horse Creek drainage. We were still at about 7,500 feet, and the sun beat down upon us like a hammer. The aid stations into Tongue River Canyon took on a Western States-like "Canyons" feel. The volunteers would rush to us and pour pitchers of freezing stream water on our heads and our upper torsos, doing all they could to bring our core temperatures down.

As we neared the bottom of Tongue River Canyon, we began passing runners from the morning's races, the 50K and the 30K, who had passed us a few hours before. The Tongue River Road led us toward the finish line in Dayton. It was a long, flat stretch of dirt road surrounded by fields of tall grass and ranch homes, each of the homes set against the land like cool, dark shadows. Instead of retreating into the shadows of their homes, the residents were out at the end of their long driveways, slapping high fives and offering garden hoses for relief. Staff at an impromptu aid station forced popsicles into our hands, which at that moment, with the afternoon temperature standing at 99 degrees, tasted like the sweet nectar of the gods.

Michelle Maneval was out along the River Road with us, with a cooler packed full of ice. She was cramming the ice in our hats, shoving it into our jog bras, filling our bottles with it, handing it out in Dixie cups like a sweet sacrament of finisher's communion. "I was like the ice fairy," she would say later of how she drove up and down the River Road in 2016, helping those who would finish on the hottest day in Bighorn's history. "We love all of our runners at Bighorn, but the people who are at the back of the pack . . . how long they're out there . . . these are like my kids to me."

As unbearably uncomfortable as the heat had become, I began to feel a sense of contentment and of belonging. This was a special moment, in a special place. My past felt like it had flooded into the present, and I could hear my footsteps moving with purpose and rhythm. I smiled and waved. The people of Tongue River Road told me I was going to make it.

"You're going to run 100 miles!" a lady called, leaning on her mailbox at the end of her driveway. "That's so unbelievable to me!"

We hustled into Dayton, crossing the town bridge across the Tongue River, then made a sharp left to the park, where hours and hours before Michelle had given her pre-race talk and her mother, Karen, had stood by, proud of her daughter, proud of her race, proud of how over the years an entire community had come together, organizers and volunteers for something larger and more meaningful than any individual, proud of what the Bighorn hundred-miler had come to represent.

I finished in 29:34. Jill welcomed me with a hug and a kiss. Katie went immediately for a swim in the cool water of the Tongue, which ran only a few yards from the finish, which was festive and fun. The smell of barbecue and burgers filled the air. Tall, majestic cottonwoods rimmed the park and provided us with protection and shade, tempering the warmth of a hot and challenging day.

A few hours later, as we sat in the incredibly spacious living room of our Sheridan College residence, a full pizza eaten, stories of our day and night and next day shared, Jill, who had been a crew chief extraordinaire, made her way to the bedroom. Katie, who had provided so much support, offering me non-stop encouragement and uplifting positive words for more than 16 hours, was curled up on the couch, fast asleep.

We had been watching TV, and the Disney Pixar film *Finding Nemo* was on. With my wife asleep in one room and my daughter asleep on the couch, I watched the final few minutes, alone in my own thoughts. I love *Finding Nemo* because its themes are so universal—of love, of letting go, and of letting things happen to those you love.

In a strange and mysterious way, Bighorn had taken me on a new path. I had allowed things to happen to me, even as I had been dogged with some inherent fears of injury and of running in a place I did not know. At a crucial juncture, I had given my race to my 23-year-old daughter and allowed her judgment to guide me home, filling me with Snickers and Coke and unconditional love. Katie loved everything about her Bighorn experience, and the love she expressed showered over me like cool water from one of those garden hoses on the long River Road back to the finish, sustaining me through those final miles.

During the course of the Bighorn 100, I had seen and experienced things that were completely new and exciting, things that were scary and challenging, things that punished me physically and moved me to awe and to tears emotionally.

The road I had traveled often, thanks to the Bighorn 100, had become a road I had seldom, if ever, traveled before. It is a road I know I will never forget, nor ever take for granted, again.

CHAPTER 11

Your Days **Are Short Here**

There are voices you hear throughout your life, voices that tend to belong to those you have learned from, voices that are memorable for their ability to see and identify the grand beauty and vast potential of other human beings. They are voices that possess a giving, generous wisdom that go along with the keen and sometimes rare perception that we often undersell what we are capable of doing, and that with the proper guidance and support, we are all capable of going the distance, that we can ask more of ourselves because there are people who see this capability lying within each of us, just waiting to be activated with a smile, an encouraging word, a belief that we can go beyond what we ever thought was possible. They are voices that evolve with the passage of time. They at first sound new and invigorating, holding the promise of new ground covered and new insight gained. As the years pass, these voices still hold their potency and retain their ability to stir you to unrealized action. But there is an added poignancy to their message.

You only have so much time left. There are only so many days remaining to fulfill the promise that the voices once saw in you. Sometimes the voices remain in your mind, but the people to whom they belonged are no longer with you. This is why so often the conversations you have with these voices as you age and as you realize the calendar is dwindling become like silent fragments. The words that stirred you were like a sermon or a speech, a decisive call to action, throughout your youth and into your middle age. Over time, however, having perhaps reached some goals but not all of them, the voices become less of a perpetual soundtrack and more of a choice. Do I really want to keep conjuring the voices and keep moving forward, still seeking out the great challenges that someone long ago said I was capable of achieving, or should I be honest with myself and acknowledge that the great enthusiasms and grand adventures of the trail are outdated? Should I put them to bed and let them rest, let them fade into the unfulfilled darkness that exists beyond memory?

Mending Fences

Antonio "Tony" Rossmann has a voice that has always sounded to me like a pen scratching thoughtfully against a piece of paper. His voice is dry and often cracks when he gets emotional. He is a person who is more defined by the thoughtful use of words, his own and the famous words of others, than anyone I've ever met. He has been a member of the board of trustees for the Western States Endurance Run for more than 30 years, serving as president of the organization in the late 1990s. As one of the top water rights and land use attorneys in the West, the Harvard-educated Tony also had the unofficial title of Western States' "counselor," guiding our organization through numerous complicated dealings with the federal government and private land holders in keeping the Western States Trail accessible and open to the public. Only recently did he receive "emeritus" status on our board, which he wrote in an email to us was one of the highlights of his life: "I first ran the race in 1985 and joined the board in 1986. I can honestly say that the Western States Endurance Run has been one of the most satisfying experiences of my years! I obviously loved the challenge of running the race and sharing the beauty of the course, but the process of protecting the race and trail for future runners with all of you is most cherished. You have been more than kind, supportive, and caring to me and my family, and I will be eternally grateful. My investment of 37 years has been far exceeded by all the benefits I have gained."

When I joined the board of trustees for Western States in 2004, one of the first people who reached out and congratulated me was Tony. He told me that my involvement with Western States was going to change my life, and he was right. What I didn't know at the time was how my friendship with Tony was also going to change how I viewed myself and what I thought I was capable of doing. I looked at his example as a past president and a key board member in an almost-covetous fashion. Few people in Western States' long history had the kind of impact Tony had on the run. I had worked for a few years as the deputy press secretary and speechwriter for Nevada Gov. Kenny Guinn, and the experience was a vivid example of how government often functions. When there were good people with good intentions like Gov. Guinn in a room, a lot could get done. Gov. Guinn had grown up poor in the Central Valley of California. His parents, who both had received very little schooling in their lives, moved to California during the Great Depression from Arkansas. Gov. Guinn had become the first person in his family to ever attend college. Eventually he became a teacher and administrator, then earned his Ph.D. and became superintendent of Las Vegas' Clark County Schools. He was the most down-to-earth, incredibly success- ful person I'd ever been around. When we'd travel to rural Nevada for a speech, we'd have to quickly round up Gov. Guinn at the high school gymnasium where he'd just spoken, or else he would linger and visit with all of the townspeople who were there, and after that, if we had failed to grab him at that point, he would then wander off to help the high school's janitor put away all of the chairs that were used for the day's event. Gov. Guinn always stressed to us that our work was never about us; it was about the people of Nevada. Gov. Guinn was a Republican, and sometimes he could get fiery if the partisan wars ever flared up. But more often than not he was a consensus-builder. He treated the leaders of the state's Democratic Party with respect. He would listen to their concerns. He would not feign interest that made for some nice head-lines but never materialized into real action. "If your word isn't your bond, then why give your word?" he would often say. He found ways to build his opponents' vision for a better Nevada into his vision for what Nevada needed to do.

Tony, a lifelong Democrat, went about his business in much the same way as Gov. Guinn. He always sought the common ground and treated everyone he met with uncommon decency. Tony got results because he was firm, but always fair, because he would actually listen and acknowledge another perspective first before he would then work backwards from that point on and would find the commonalities that could lead to an equitable solution for all parties involved.

Nowhere was this more apparent than the heroic lobbying effort Tony made during the late 1980s to keep a key section of the Western States Trail open when it was in danger of being cut off from the public. The 1984 California Wilderness Act enacted by Congress created numerous federally protected wilderness areas in the state, including the Granite Chief Wilderness, which runs for approximately four miles on the early portions of the Western States Endurance Run's course. The Granite Chief deserved this protection in every way. Managed by the Tahoe National Forest, the more than 25,000 acres of the Granite Chief is one glacier-carved valley after another, the drainages of which form the headwaters of the Middle Fork of the American River, where dramatic granite outcroppings that reach more than 9,000 feet in elevation stare down at vast green meadows lined by old growth red fir, aspens, and mule's ears. The 1984 Wilderness Act also made it clear that events like the Western States Run and the Tevis Cup Ride, with their hundreds of competitors and additional impacts of volunteers, aid stations, and medical checks, were not in the spirit of the untrammeled, and non-mechanized, nature of protected wilderness areas like the Granite Chief. A compromise of some sort needed to be reached. Tony, in his wire-framed glasses and trademark bow tie, made numerous trips to Washington, D.C., working to convince the members of California's congressional delegation that the Granite Chief Wilderness, even with its protected status, should remain open to the run and the ride. In 1988, Congress and the Forest Service granted permission for the Western States Endurance Run to continue in perpetuity its historic use of the trail within the Granite Chief Wilderness Area. As part of the compromise that was brokered, a limit was placed on the number of entrants Western States could admit into each year's event: 369 runners. Twenty years later, still working on keeping the trail open, Tony helped negotiate the sale of Pointed Rocks Ranch, a 370-acre property where a section of Western States' latter stages run through, to California State Parks. The transaction protected the "Pointed Rocks" section of the course where today the 95-mile mark of the Western States course is located.

When I became president of Western States in 2010 and throughout my tenure, which lasted until 2015, I learned how Tony was able to record these complex achievements. He had an incredibly agile mind, one that throughout his career in law had never been completely stumped by even the most vexing of problems. He could quote all of the writings of the U.S. Supreme Court Justices. His handiwork and influence were evident in water use and rights decisions made by the courts throughout the West. He represented Inyo County and the Friends of Mammoth throughout their decades-long battle to regain control of the local water resources and reclaim the environment that had been devastated when water was diverted decades earlier from the Eastern Sierra to the city of Los Angeles. He told me once, "You deal with any tough issue with rigor as well as respect, with integrity, and intellectual honesty."

Tony knew the law as well as anyone. He also understood people. He was always the person who reminded us to be better, to act better, to treat others better. I can still remember a tense meeting with the Forest Service and the Ride. A trail disagreement had broken out. There was misunderstanding between the run and the ride about how best to maintain the Western States Trail through trail work. The run preferred low-impact methods like hand tools. The ride had used a more high-impact trail machine that worked more quickly but left a disturbance in its wake. A meeting was called. I was serving as our president at the time. I was afraid that the bad feelings and harsh words that had been exchanged on the trail in the weeks prior between our two groups might arise when we all sat in a room together. In the parking lot, outside the meeting, Tony walked up to me. He grabbed both of my hands. He looked me deep in the eye.

"Everything is going to be OK," he said, sensing my unease. Then he smiled. Tony always has had this calming way of maintaining a decent firmness. He kept holding my hands in his. His voice was a carpet of many colors, fatherly yet determined, sweet, calm, and wise. "You're going to be OK. You're going to do great. Remember there are no enemies, only adversaries, which carries the opportunity for peace and elegant solutions."

And, as we walked into the meeting room, before I had a chance to convene our meeting or even sit down, Tony walked directly from me to the other side of the room. He sought out Kathie Perry, the former ride president and past Tevis Cup champion. He greeted Kathie warmly, like the old friend that she was, with a hug. He sought out the barrel-chested Tom Christofk and recalled the work they had done together when Tony was president of the run and Tom was the president of the ride. Tony then proceeded to wrap Tom's imposing, prideful chest in a runner's hug that Tom couldn't escape. "It's good to see you, Tony," Tom said.

These were people who had relationships with Tony that went back decades. The message was clear. The ride and run had a history together. Yes, there was a challenging conversation still to come about mending the relationship between the ride and the run, but that was OK. We all came, whether it was the ride or the run, from the very beginning when Wendell Robie and Dru Barner and others liked them saw that there could be both. We shared a history. We had worked together. The confrontation I feared and any bad blood that I was worried about had dissipated even before any of us had even sat down at the conference table, all simply because Tony chose decency over dissent, goodwill over grievance, collaboration over conflict.

We worked things out that day. We mended fences and moved on.

Navigating the Unexpected

During the Western States weekend before Tony suffered a stroke in 2017, I spent a lot of time with him. We ate dinner with some friends the night before that year's race in a crowded restaurant in the village at Olympic Valley, only a few hundred yards from the next morning's start line. Tony was full of reflections about past races, past travels throughout the country where he had run other ultras—he had a fondness for

Leadville founder Ken Chlouber's rugged individualism—as well as the relationships he had managed, sometimes successfully and sometimes not so successfully, throughout his life. He mentioned how he thought he hadn't been a very understanding partner when he was younger, and it wasn't until he met Kathy, his wife of more than 25 years and the mother of their college-aged twin daughters, Molly and Alice, that he'd come to realize that it was people like Kathy (an incredibly bright and accomplished professional herself) who can help a person take an additional step in understanding who they need to be. "I thought I was complete but was utterly incomplete until I met Kathy," Tony said. He looked to me, and our other dinner companion, Dr. Gary Towle, another longtime Western States board member, and smiled. "Gentlemen, whenever we are lucky enough to marry someone who can take us on the path of making us one day whole, it's one of the life's true miracles, isn't it?" As we called it a night, a bleary-eyed 3:30 a.m. wake-up awaiting us all in preparation for the 5 a.m. start, Tony mentioned that he had been blessed to know so many good people through his association with Western States. He gave me a hug and planted a gentle, fatherly, Italian-style kiss on my cheek as we parted ways that night.

A few days later, we received the word that Tony, who had traveled back East with Kathy right after Western States to be with Molly, who was preparing for her junior year at Dartmouth College, had suffered a major stroke. He was eventually moved to a rehabilitation hospital in Boston, then returned to his home in Oakland a few months later. He had lost mobility on one side and was in a wheelchair. He also for a time lost almost all of his ability to speak. Through unceasing and determined work with speech specialists, he has regained the ability to say some short sentences. Whenever you are with him, Tony is completely attentive and aware of all that you are saying to him. Perhaps it is a function of being almost 80 years old and being thankful for the life that he has lived, but he also has cried at one point or another during every visit I've had with him since his stroke. I like to think about Tony's tears as a manifestation of a person grateful for the live he has lived. Indeed, Tony has lived a life where he has done much and given to others so much more.

And when I hear his voice today, it is always the same. Until Tony suffered his stroke, it was always his duty and his profound privilege to get on the microphone in the shade of the popup tents that come to resemble a small city on the infield of Placer High School on Sunday afternoon when the finishers and their families and friends gather in that cool shade for the awards presentation of the finisher's buckles. Tony would read with careful calibration each finisher's name and finishing time, sometimes more than 300 names in all. And then he would conclude the ceremony with sage words that were spoken long ago, from a speech originally given to the senior class of Princeton University in the spring of 1954, by Adlai Stevenson, the two-time Democratic Party nominee for president and the governor of Illinois:

"Your days are short here; this is the last of your springs. And now in the serenity and quiet of this lovely place, touch the depths of truth, feel the hem of heaven. You will go away with old, good friends. And don't forget when you leave, why you came."

It is a voice that will always sound to me like a pen scratching thoughtfully against a piece of paper. It is a voice that, even with the passage of time, will remain clear and vivid to me, reminding me to never forget that when it is my time to leave, I should always remember and be eternally grateful for, the purpose of why I came.

Holding Fast to Dreams

In addition to the voices that we hear, there are the dreams that we all have, some that are impossible to attain, some that remain well within our grasp. In 2021, I attempted, along with Katie, to complete the Grand Slam of ultra running. Katie completed the four hundred-milers in the space of the summer's 99 days. I made it through two and a half of them. I finished Old Dominion among the picture-postcard green hills of the Shenandoah Valley in early June with 25 minutes to spare before the cutoff. Three weeks later, I returned to Western States and had my own Golden Hour glory, finishing with so many whoops of joy that my throat hurt for the next week, in 29:42. And then we traveled in August to Leadville for the third leg of the Grand Slam. I had finished Leadville in 2013 and knew from that experience how much the constant effort at the 10,000-foot and above altitude could take a toll on you. In July, I drove to Leadville's Sugar Loafin' campground and conducted a mini training camp of three days to prepare. Katie joined me for two of the days, and on one of them, we made our way up 12,600-foot Hope Pass. As we moved above the tree line, the sky darkened so quickly there was little time for us to react. The wind began whipping and rain began pelting us with such force, we could barely maintain our balance. Katie ran ahead of me and made it to the top of Hope, where there is a mound of rocks and prayer flags to commemorate an astounding view of Leadville hemmed in on all sides by the rocky shoulders of 14,000-foot mountain peaks. I joined Katie a few minutes later. As we stood in the whipping wind, the rain pelting our faces like hard pebbles, I had a hard time imagining in the matter of a few weeks having to climb up Hope Pass, then over and down its rugged and rutted backside to the abandoned mining town of Winfield, then climbing back up and over Hope again. Such an exercise felt ridiculously excessive. If the biblical weather conditions of this day of having just run up one side of Hope Pass hadn't killed me, surely running up both sides of Hope Pass on race day would.

As it turned out, Hope Pass would prove to be the crux of my Leadville 100 experience. It was late in the afternoon of race day as

I made my way down the backside of Hope Pass. I knew I didn't have very much time left to make the 6 p.m. cutoff at the 50-mile turnaround at the old mining settlement of Winfield. I'd seen Katie already. She'd made the turn, had come out of the aid station tents at Winfield, and was in great spirits as she prepared to make the 2,500-foot climb back up to Hope Pass. I was still almost two miles from Winfield when we met on the trail. She was coming, and I was still going. She gave me a hug and encouraged me: "You've got this. You can do it!"

A summer of Grand Slam running was on the line. I hustled into Winfield. One of the volunteers, a young woman who calmly and assuredly told me, "You've still got time," grabbed my hydration vest bladder, started filling it and, like an experienced checker at a grocery store, handed me a Zip-Loc bag to fill with food. I had less than two minutes to get out of the aid station before the 50-mile cutoff time. A tall young man named Boaz helped me. He carried some of my stuff as I started to sprint for the timing mat out of the aid station. I've never had such a short distance feel so long. I crossed it with about 28 seconds to spare before the 6 p.m. cutoff. The entire aid station erupted in wild cheering. I raised my hands in the air. It felt like I'd just won.

"You made it," Boaz cried.

"I did!" I yelled. "I made it!"

It's not often you can say in one breath that you made it, knowing full well that in the next you aren't going to make it. But that was Leadville briefly for me. It was an imperfect day with dead legs, a touchy stomach, and moments I thought I couldn't go on. But it was also, strangely and cosmically, a day where I stubbornly kept going on even when the hard reality told me I shouldn't. It was a day that I might not have been able to see and experience things I could have never dreamed or imagined. The first was climbing back up the backside Hope Pass after my escape from Winfield in the faint half-light of a day that hadn't gone as planned. I knew full well there was no way I could get back to Twin Lakes at mile 60 in time for the next cutoff. I wasn't alone with this realization. I had been the last runner out of Winfield. But quickly I came upon others like myself. Earlier we were like a bunch of excited butterflies, all of us a fluttering frenzy of excitement as we had beaten the cutoff at Winfield. There was now a crushing enormity before us as the trail straightened stiffly and steeply above us. Our task was to keep moving. But our even deeper task was to tell ourselves that to keep moving was somehow worth it, knowing that somehow the trail math just wouldn't add up. The sound of our labored breathing and the impending darkness, how I saw my fellow runners swaying with weakness as they fought to find more oxygen as we spied the jagged end of the tree line, pushing ourselves to go on, reminded me of our promised mission: to keep moving.

There was a dark-haired woman in tights and jacket and gloves sitting on one of the boulders. I'd heard her gasping for air for the last several hundred yards. She looked at me, her expression pained and perplexed, wondering how we've gotten into this place here on the side of this mountain, the climb still endless, with, really, no more hope of making the next cutoff.

"We're going to keep going until someone has to tell us we can't, right?" I said to her. I was surprised by my sudden burst of jaunty enthusiasm. I'm not even sure I believed my own words. But the dark-haired woman looked at me like my words touched her deeply and reminded her of something. Her expression, which seemed lost, brightened.

"Yeah baby!" she said, sounding even more enthusiastic than I had sounded earlier. She straightened and lifted herself from the boulder. She had to catch her balance for a second, but then she was moving again. I could hear deep and labored breathing behind me. She went on.

Later, I took a look behind me. The mountains that encircle Winfield several miles below us were unlike any other mountains I've ever seen. The trail below us has been softened like a moist potato peel by rains from thunderous clouds from earlier in the day. But even as I stopped to take in the view and perhaps find a moment of peace, I was reminded that finding reverie at Leadville takes work. I stood on the moist trail to lean forward, the pitch to the top still so steep I had to be careful not to fall backwards. The mountains behind us, though, were lovely and incomparably unassailable, their proud slopes nearly non-existent. The impending darkness was like a dramatic overture that played across them in a kind of silent roar, giving them even greater dimension and meaning. We battled the mountains and the high altitude of Leadville all day. We weren't going to experience the finish line that had loftily inhabited our dreams this summer. Yet we were determined, all of us, to keep moving.

And we did. I looked back one last time near the top of Hope Pass and see a line of headlamps below me, like a stubborn string of old Christmas lights that you thought you had thrown out but find each December tucked away somewhere in your garage. Our reason to believe, our reason to keep going, even if it was no longer in an official finish, remained. About two hours later, I struggled across the Arkansas River for the final time. I was dazed and tired, and the cold water of the Arkansas cut through me like the chilled hand of a ghost. After about three or four calls from the darkness, I heard a familiar voice. Jeffrey Conner, my pacer, was there to greet me. I had missed the Twin Lakes cutoff by more than an hour. But Jeffrey, as he always does, smiled. He praised my effort. We hugged on the rocky banks of a chilly river that murmured with the challenge of life under the vivid light of a full moon. My race was ending. But it still felt alive with purpose to me. You hold onto a dream long enough, particularly through an entire summer of dreams, you never want to wake up. You never want to let it go.

Not long after, we reached the trailhead at Twin Lakes. In the near-empty parking lot, I saw the rest of our crew: Jill, our friends Kathie Maestas and Lauren Watson. Lauren was to pace Katie later at Outward Bound aid station for the final 23 miles. There were long hugs and words of thanks and encouragement. I thought about how lucky I am to know and love such wonderful people. I told each of them that. When my wrist band was cut, any disappointment I might have felt that my Grand Slam summer was over was replaced immediately instead by an abiding sense of pride. I thought about how lucky I was to have seen and experienced all that this summer had been.

For some reason, I thought of Leadville in terms of how it seems so much like when you are born. How its majestic mountains can reduce us to something very basic and elemental. How we come into this life screaming and struggling for our first breaths, and how during the course of this 100-mile race our challenge becomes something very similar. There are moments where we literally are searching for the reasons to keep going, to keep fighting, to keep breathing, to find the underlying reasons why life is worth every moment we have the privilege to possess it. The mountains of Leadville, even in their supreme beauty, remind us all how small we really are. And, if we are lucky, their refined transparence that fills this moon-filled night with a ghostly and otherworldly presence that seems to be whispering of those who have come before you, might come to include something more. These mountains might come to include the remains of this day: those whose strides and steps, sometimes mortally slow and sometimes swift as gods, those who made it the entire 100-mile distance back to the town of Leadville where the finish line awaited.

Jeffrey and I stood on a rise maybe a half mile from the finish line at Sixth and Harrison in Leadville. For the past half hour, the finishers of the Leadville 100 came by us in all forms and in all fashions. Some were still bundled from head to toe in their night gear, as the wind of night had swept across the grassy prairie-like field near Outward Bound or the chilled ghostly voices of the early morning hours had crept along with them on the shores of Turquoise Lake with only a half-marathon to go. Some had stripped back down to their shorts and T-shirts like it was a 90-degree day rather than the 50-ish degrees we were experiencing on this crisp August morning. Some were buoyant, surrounded by pacers, friends, and family. A mustached runner had a group of girls all wearing reasonable facsimiles of his black mustache on their faces. The girls followed behind him in joyful and playful song. Their singing had him smiling like a dad gently taking a minivan full of his daughters and their friends to soccer practice. Others moved much more slowly and gingerly, the full 100-mile distance exhibiting its elusiveness and its difficulty, their steps seemingly arthritic, bent, deliberate, and exhausted but still determined to reach the red carpet leading to the Leadville finish line.

We soon saw Katie and Lauren cresting the hill. They smiled and pointed. We smiled, pointed, and added excited yells. They returned our excited yells with yells of their own. I could already feel my throat fill with emotion. This was Katie's third 100-mile finish of the summer, her third Grand Slam race of four. When she and Lauren reached us, Katie said she was tired. But our reunion was the stuff of excitement and love and the expectation of grand tales and stories that will be told over and over for years to come. We made our way to the finish down Sixth Street. The crowd swelled as we saw the streetlight at Harrison Avenue looming like a blinking red holy grail. Soon we could barely hear one another, the cheering was so loud. I could see Katie beginning to half-smile, half-tear up. Jeffrey and I fell behind and to the side to give Katie and Lauren their finishing moment. But Katie would have none of it. This is a story that will be written and shared with the most special of finishes—a finish of us together. She motioned Jeffrey and I back to her side. We crossed the finish line together. For the first time since I raised my hands in the air in triumph after sprinting madly like my life depended on it out of Winfield with 28 seconds to spare, I raised my hands in the air again. This time, instead of the uncertainty of what would happen next, the feeling was one of pure triumph.

Soon Jill and Kathie were with us. Cole Chlouber, son of Leadville founder Ken Chlouber, greeted Katie. Cole's rousing pre-run talk on Friday at the Lake County High School football field brought the runners to their feet. He talked about digging deep, how taking one step would lead to another and then another until finally a runner would find his or her way back up and over the backside hopelessness of Hope Pass back to Twin Lakes and on to the rich rewards of the finish at Sixth and Harrison. Cole wasn't exaggerating. It was exactly what Katie has done for a little more than 29 hours. Cole's speech would've made Cole's daddy Ken, having to stay in Denver this weekend due to blood clots in his lungs, proud. Cole hugged Katie. His veined arms draped a finisher's medal around her neck. He handed her a pink rose—a race tradition that his daddy's longtime race partner, Merilee Maupin, instituted years ago to celebrate the amazing and strong women who finish Leadville.

I've dreamt of the Leadville finish line a lot this summer. I've felt in my restless dreams during this summer of running hundred-mile races throughout the country the thrill of running those last few yards over the Leadville's red finish carpet. A Leadville finish was to be a springboard to Wasatch and the completion of the Grand Slam. I can honestly say not one dream I've had this summer about finishing Leadville ever ended this way. Not one, for some strange reason that was actually borne out in our first two Grand Slam races where Katie finished ahead of me by several hours, ever included me finishing with Katie. Maybe it was too special of a finish to ever imagine, too elusive, too precious, and too rare to ever call a dream.

I didn't make it. Yet I did make it. I joined my daughter. I crossed the Leadville finish line with her. A day of chasing cutoffs ended the next morning with us together. This moment, deafened by supportive cheers that pierced a robin's egg blue Leadville sky with the very best emotion that humans can ever display, standing near my daughter who found her way up and over and up and over again the special mountains of which she will now forever be a part, was better than any dream I could have ever had.

Somehow, it feels like this was how it was all meant to be. The dreams we possess we don't ever actually own. If they are to be true dreams, dreams that matter, we must share them with others. Whenever we do, the races that we run will never seem as long. Whenever we do, we guarantee that we are always running toward something that truly matters. Whenever we run, we should always run toward life.

Acknowledgments

If not for a plane ride in February 2022, when a few of us accompanied our friend Kathie Maestas to the Rocky Raccoon hundred-miler in Huntsville, Texas, and we happened to run into another friend, Vicky Vaughn Shea, on our flight, I don't know if this book would've ever been written. Vicky, one of the best book designers in the country and one of the nicest people you will ever meet, was on her way to a book convention in Denver. She was also a member of our running group in Reno. She was coming back from knee replacement surgery, and eventually that weekend would have dinner with a couple of old book industry colleagues of hers, Jennifer Dorsey and Vanessa Campos. Jennifer and Vanessa's Broad Book Press publishes numerous titles throughout each year, but more than that, they provide the right amount of positive energy, encouragement, and hope to writers who feel they have a book in them. All of us had spoken about another book project before the pandemic. In Denver, Vicky, Jen, and Vanessa discussed the possibility of another possible book project. This book happened because of that conversation. I cannot thank Vicky enough for her constant friendship and her championing of my writing, and Jen and Vanessa for believing that I indeed had a book in me that might be worth reading.

This book also owes a debt of gratitude to the publishers and editors of *Ultra Running Magazine*. Since 2015, I've written a regular column for *UR*, "The Voice of the Sport," and I've contributed to the magazine for an even longer period than that, for nearly two decades now. Publishers Karl Hoagland and "Tropical" John Medinger, editors Tia Bodington, Erika Hoagland, and most importantly the current *UR* editor, Amy Clark (who has become a great friend), have all encouraged me to write the stories of the great people who inhabit the sport of ultra running. I am eternally grateful for the opportunity *UR* has always provided me.

Finally, I need to thank my family and friends. I am incredibly blessed to be a part of numerous families. There is the Western States family, of which I became an unofficial member back in 1987 when I first covered Western States as a young journalist. I became a more official member of the WS family when I ran the race for the first time in 1997, and finally, such an official family member that I've served on the race's board of trustees since 2004. I have gained so much from all of the people who have made Western States such a special and life-affirming event.

There is also my "Strider Family," the folks of our running group here in Reno, the Silver State Striders, who I've run with, raced with, crewed for, paced for, volunteered with, and generally shared life with for more than two decades. I've never met a better mixture of people who embody in every way what it means to help, to give, to share, and to love more than the Striders. And finally, thanks can't even begin to do justice to what my wife, Jill, and my two daughters, Annie and Katie, have meant to me. I knew more than 35 years ago I had found a keeper in Jill when I dragged her all over the Western States course while I was covering the race for the very first time. It was a hot and exhausting day. But Jill never complained, and she was there with me the entire time. If I had never met Jill, the events in this book would have never happened. Her constancy and her encouragement to always keep moving, to always run another day, and her belief in me have never wavered. And in Annie and Katie I have two of the most wonderful and interesting trail companions a runner could ever have. Over time, I've learned so much from both of my daughters—to care and to be genuinely interested in others, to have fun and to not worry so much, to dig deep and always finish the thing that you've started.

To all of these people, and so many others, thank you.

About the Author

John Trent is a former two-time Nevada Sportswriter of the Year who lives in Reno, Nevada, with his ultra-running family: wife Jill and daughters Annie and Katie. A past president of the Western States Endurance Run and member of Western States' board of trustees since 2004, he has been involved with ultra running as an organizer, volunteer, participant, and journalist covering the sport since 1987.

DEAR READER,

We hope you enjoyed reading *Running Toward Life* as much as we enjoyed working on it. In the course of going through the stories with John we realized that there were so many more stories to share that these pages just couldn't hold. The solution in this modern age of technology was simple, a mini series of podcast episodes.

We are proud to present the Running Toward Life Podcast series. Listen to John as he interviews elite runners and Western States Endurance Run finishers including Tim Twietmeyer, Craig Thornley, Clare Gallagher, Brittany Peterson, and the first race co-directors Mo Livermore and Shannon Weil.

Scan the QR code below or visit bit.ly/runningtowardlifepodcast

See you on the trail,
The Broad Book Group Team

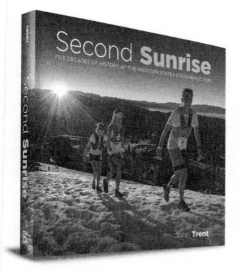

MORE FROM JOHN TRENT

Second Sunrise: Five Decades of History at the Western States Endurance Run

Since its founding in 1974, Western States had also been predicated on the notion that in the beginning at the first sunrise, as the run begins at 5 a.m., there must always be hope that 100 miles was within a runner's grasp. And then, with the start of a second sunrise, there had to be continued determination to search out where the finish still might lie. Even if the clock ran out, the second sunrise would not fail you. The hope of a second sunrise would always be enough to get you to the finish.

To learn more, scan the QR code below or visit bit.ly/secondsunrise

Second Sunrise is published in collaboration with Ponderosa Pine Design, Broad Book Press, and with the support of the Western States® 100-Mile Endurance Run.